In Praise of Meekness

IN PRAISE OF MEEKNESS

Essays on Ethics and Politics

NORBERTO BOBBIO

Translated by Teresa Chataway

Polity

Copyright © this translation Polity Press 2000

First published in Italy as *Elogio della Mitezza e altri scritti morali* © Nuova Pratiche Editrice, Milano 1998.

First published in 2000 by Polity Press in association with Blackwell Publishers Ltd.
Published with the assistance of the Italian Ministry of Foreign Affairs.

Editorial office:
Polity Press
65 Bridge Street
Cambridge CB2 1UR, UK

Marketing and production:
Blackwell Publishers Ltd
108 Cowley Road
Oxford OX4 1JF, UK

Published in the USA by
Blackwell Publishers Inc.
Commerce Place
350 Main Street
Malden, MA 02148, USA

A catalogue record for this book is available from the British Library.

Library of Congress Cataloging-in-Publication Data

Bobbio, Norberto, 1909–
    [Elogio della mitezza e altri scritti morali. English]
    In praise of meekness: essays on ethics and politics/Norberto Bobbio; translated by Teresa Chataway.
        p. cm.
    Includes bibliographical references.
    ISBN 0–7456–2308–5 (hc)—ISBN 0–7456–2309–3 (pb)
    1. Political ethics. I. Title.

JA79 .B56 2000
172—dc21

Typeset in 11 on 13 pt Berling
by Kolam Information Services Pvt. Ltd, Pondicherry, India.
Printed in Great Britain by T. J. International, Padstow, Cornwall

This book is printed on acid-free paper.

Contents

Translator's Preface

The Italian philosopher Norberto Bobbio (b. 1909) is well known for his moral reflections and role as a mediating intellectual. For him, morals and politics are two mutually incompatible ethics that govern us. They exist because neither alone is sufficient to guarantee both civil coexistence and survival.[1] Morals, or the ethics of principles, do not guarantee survival. Politics, or the ethics of useful outcomes, do not guarantee civil coexistence. From this antinomy emerge the particular situations that form our daily experience, which he calls 'cases of conscience'.[2] For Bobbio, democracy is the political system that allows the closest proximity between the needs of morals and those of politics. Such a relationship ought to indicate the direction in which one must move to render the form of democratic government increasingly closer to its ideal.

This is the first time a number of his essays on morals and ethics have appeared in English.[3] For political philosophers and theorists, his work on what he terms 'the lessons of the classics' and 'preferred authors', his 'lifetime of research' on democracy, rights, peace, and the left and right political spectrum, is now readily available in English.[4] To illustrate, his *Left and Right: The Significance of a Political Distinction* argument has recently been favourably referred to in Giddens's *The Third Way*.[5]

Bobbio's interpretation of the contribution of less well-known Italian thinkers to the political and ethical climate of that country is also available.[6] It is not generally known in the

English-speaking world that he spent almost forty years of his life teaching legal philosophy and theory. Only a few of his numerous legal writings are available in English. They include a piece on 'law and force',[7] a commentary on trends in Italian legal theory of the 1960s,[8] and an essay on 'the promotion of action in the modern state'.[9] Two pieces, one on 'Reason in law',[10] the other his opening address to the seventeenth IVR World Congress, 'Challenges to law at the end of the 20th century', in Bologna (16–21 June 1995),[11] have appeared in the legal journal *Ratio Juris*. As well, there is his recent discussion on the importance of Hans Kelsen to the international legal system.[12] Clearly a lacuna exists in the availability in English of the extent of his contribution to legal philosophy. However, the legal-political nexus in his thought becomes readily apparent in the above-cited political writings, and in part in these moral essays.[13] On the existence of that nexus he is absolutely clear:

> I cannot forget that I devoted some of my later studies to the question of the relation between law and power. This is a subject which I somewhat regarded as the conclusion of that dual experience, as a scholar of both legal and political philosophy, of studies in political theory which are grafted onto the prior ones in legal theory.[14]

To date, his moral philosophy reveals itself in many of his contributions to the Turinese daily *La Stampa*, in whose pages since 1976 he has written many reflexive and provocative pieces as interventions in what he terms 'the contingent polemic'.[15] The most famous is 'L'utopia capovolta' ('The upturned utopia')[16] written during the collapse of historical communism, and republished soon after in the *New Left Review*.[17] Since then it has been included in collections on the 1989 experience, and beyond. Consistent with his goal of developing informed democratic citizens, he also uses the pages of *La Stampa* to create debates in the public conscience. His most recent foray is expressing through that and other papers his view of NATO's illegal involvement in Kosovo.

Given his major contribution to intellectual debates in Italy for the past sixty years, it is timely that this third dimension of his philosophical endeavour now becomes available as essays on ethics and politics. They revisit his political and legal foundations, and without crowding out his moral and ethical perspectives, provide an informative background to his particular line of reasoning as a man of moderation. The influence of what he terms 'the lesson of the classics' (from Aristotle and Plato, the Reformation writers and Enlightenment thinkers)[18] and 'recurrent topics' (such as 'Are politicians moral?', 'Are Italians racist?', and 'Is there a God?') enhance his perspective. For different reasons, the influence of Vilfredo Pareto, Gaetano Mosca, Carl Schmitt and Hans Kelsen is also revealed. The depth of his scholarship becomes readily apparent in his use of some less familiar early philosophers to make telling points. Of interest, too, is his use of modern European intellectuals (Elias Canetti, Michael Foucault, Paul Ricoeur, Gerhard Ritter, Ignazio Silone, and Leonardo Sciascia) and Anglo-American theorists (Alasdair MacIntyre, Felix Oppenheim, and Amartya Sen). These avenues of exploration reveal him to be both a European and a universalist.

Finally, there is Bobbio's writing style. He has a longstanding interest in linguistic analysis and 'issues of words'.[19] Characteristically, his writings are excursions in thought, and models of analysis and interpretation. Structurally, his style is based on classical logic in that he constructs his argument by defining, explaining, and concluding. Methodologically, he employs a critical spirit to draw attention to particular issues to be confronted. Because his central aim is to communicate, and conscious of the complexity of the issues he often addresses, he strives to reduce that complexity through an expressive prose, free as much as possible from colloquialisms, rhetoric, and esoteric terms. Using a variety of skills, often at a key point he will ask a question, prompting the reader to deal with what is being stated, to evaluate, reply, and then follow on for an answer that may advance the argument. Such questions help to maintain the reader's alertness. A question may be answered in the ensuing sentence, or only after a further involved exposition. Sometimes an answer important to the whole discussion will still require further consideration by the other side. This is yet another aspect of his didactic method. For a fruitful reading it is essential to approach Bobbio's work without preconceptions and ingrained notions about certain meanings, in order to capture what he is conveying through words such as truth, tolerance, justice, equality, rights, prejudice, dissent, tyranny, and nonviolence.

Three clear features of the mature Bobbio become apparent from these essays. First, with his introduction, he sheds some of his avowed 'self-doubts' about the relevance of his moral philosophy and perspectives. He once wrote that 'I regard myself as belonging to the group of the "never happy". I am a man of doubt... [and] I do not find writing easy. Everything that I write costs me great effort, an effort which generally seems to me greater than the results.'[20] That doubt emerged in the early 1950s as Italy's democratic Republic gradually stabilized, and he engaged in consequential debates with the communists. His self-doubt re-emerged in the late 1960s with increased violence and terrorism in Italy, and was compounded by the student revolution. It came to the fore again in the early 1980s when, during a prolific writing phase after his formal retirement from teaching, he seriously questioned the validity of a range of his positions. In a recent dialogue with Perry Anderson, he once again raises that self-doubt: 'I have never been very sure of myself. Now, less than ever.'[21] Interestingly, there is relatively little of that self-questioning in these selected essays. They can be viewed as signposts as he guides himself through the growing maturity of his reflections. Overall, they represent an affirmation of 'why' and to a lesser extent 'how' he arrives at such positive chiliastic expectations, to use the expression of one of his preferred authors, Kant.[22]

Second, the essays provide a line of reasoning in his moral philosophy over time, and its concurrent development with his political thought. The earliest essay, 'Truth and liberty', was drafted during his debate with Palmiro Togliatti and other communist intellectuals during the 1950s, and was included in his seminal *Politica e cultura* (1955). That issue of truthfulness in both public and private spheres has dominated his perspectives since then, and it is a theme that re-emerges in his exhortations for transparent government, one in which secrecy has no place. From the distinctly Italian political milieu during the 1950s to the 1970s he translated that generic thinking on 'truth and liberty' by addressing civil society questions arising in the 1980s and 1990s. These questions cover the extent to which meekness (which he first wrote about in 1983), ethics (1983 and 1984), and nonviolence and the democratic state (1991) interface with public sphere activity. With the increasing cosmopolitanism in Italy and beyond,[23] those thematic issues have been tested against the emergence of prejudice (1979), tolerance and truth (1988), and attitudes to racism (1993). These essays, commencing with the overarching 'In praise of meekness', are dyadically linked in four sections and an appendix. Bobbio shows us that they have political, legal, *and* moral implications which cannot be compartmentalized. They are comprehensively interwoven. Solutions can only be found through interdisciplinary perspectives that accommodate each other, and out of which perhaps a demonstrably aware and sharing community might emerge. This is the reason why he has chosen a man of moderation, Erasmus with his Christian humanism, as an ideal model. His virtue was meekness, and while never a man of action, he held religious fanaticism and the *libido dominandi* of princes to be the enemies of peace. He was never satisfied with anything he wrote.

Third, the vertex of Bobbio's moral philosophy is to be found in the last essay, 'The gods that failed' (1994), and in his debates with other interlocutors through the pages of *La Stampa* (both 1989). It comes as no real surprise that, aged ninety, and for most of his life having been a non-believer thoroughly respectful of the place faith has in other people's lives, he reveals himself in such a reflexive and 'lighthearted' way. He has some misgivings about his beliefs, and uses others' observations, ranging from a local Catholic bishop to the Jewish philosopher Hans Jonas (1903–93),[24] to challenge his iteratively developed views. The result is a contemplative freshness that characterizes his current public debates and writings, particularly on the Kosovo crisis, the development of the International Criminal Court, the international legal system and the United Nations, and legal international democratization.

In regard to these three features, the non-Italian reader is of course at a peculiar disadvantage. A translator is inexorably forced to choose among many aspects of connotation for particular words, and to recast sentences into a very different mould. Parallel words and even rather lengthy phrases have sometimes been used to render single Italian words and colloquialisms in order to convey adequately their breadth of meaning. Throughout these essays every attempt has been made to maintain consistency in the translation of given words, to reduce the gender specificity intrinsic to the Italian language, and to mirror as faithfully as possible the internal emphases of construction resident in the Italian text. Yet despite all such efforts, there are limits to the degree that the evocative power of the original text, and often the original stress and turn of phrase, can be preserved for the English-speaking reader. It needs to be added that perhaps a key problem for such readers is apt to lie, not in reading Bobbio in translation, but in encountering words which although familiar must be allowed to come through with fresh meaning. Usually definition and context can provide considerable assistance. In effect, the whole process rests on the level of receptivity and genuine critical analysis we are prepared to devote to such writings.

This translation was made easier by Bobbio's clarification of a number of issues, especially those distinctly esoteric to Italy but capable of being conveyed to a wider audience. As Umberto Eco states, 'Perhaps the Pure Language does not exist, but pitting one language against another is a splendid adventure, and it is not necessarily true, as the Italian saying goes, that the *translator* is always a *traitor*. Provided that the author takes part in this admirable treason.'[25] Since 1992 I have benefited from a continuing intellectual involvement with Bobbio's writings, and conducted extensive in-depth interviews with him on his philosophical underpinnings.[26] He has been unfailingly helpful in clarifying uncertainties during the final stages of this translation. Thus Bobbio has been part of both the 'splendid adventure' and the 'admirable treason'.[27]

Teresa Chataway
Australian Research Council Postdoctoral Fellow
Institute for Social Research
Swinburne University
Melbourne

Notes

Unless otherwise cited, all references are to Bobbio. Throughout this translation, where possible an English translation of foreign-language titles has been provided in the notes, even though there may be no equivalent English publication. The exceptions are those instances where the Italian and English expression is quite similar, or the reference is to a minor article.

1. 'Morale e politica al bivio' ['Morals and politics at the cross-roads'], *La Stampa* (1991), 5 February.
2. N. Bobbio, 'Morale e politica: due codici differenti ma necessari', ['Morals and politics: two different but necessary codes'], *La Stampa* (1979), 6 March. For a more extended discussion on this topic, see his 'Politics and morality' in E. Gellner and C. Cansino (eds) *Liberalism in Modern Times* (Budapest, Central European University Press 1996), p. 143.
3. His first English writing is *The Philosophy of Decadentism* (Oxford, Blackwell 1948).
4. See his *The Future of Democracy* (1987), *Which Socialism?* (1987), *Democracy and Dictatorship* (1989), *The Age of Rights* (1996), and *Left and Right: The Significance of a Political Distinction* (1996), all Polity Press. There are also his *Liberalism and Democracy* (London, Verso 1990) and *Thomas Hobbes and the Natural Law Tradition* (Chicago, University of Chicago Press 1993).
5. A. Giddens, *The Third Way: The Renewal of Social Democracy* (Cambridge, Polity Press 1998), pp. 38–41.
6. *Ideological Profile of Twentieth-Century Italy* (Princeton NJ, Princeton University Press 1995).
7. 'Law and force', *Monist* (1965), XLIX(3), July, pp. 321–41.
8. 'Trends in Italian legal theory', *American Journal of Comparative Law* (1959), VIII, Summer, pp. 329–40.

9. 'The promotion of action in the modern state', in G. Hughes (ed.), *Law, Reason and Justice: Essays in Legal Philosophy* (New York University Press 1969), pp. 189–206.
10. 'Reason in law', *Ratio Juris* (1988), pp. 97–108.
11. 'An autobiographical aperçu of legal philosophy', *Ratio Juris* (1996), 9(2), pp. 121–4.
12. (with Danilo Zolo), 'Hans Kelsen: the theory of law and the international legal system. A talk', *European Journal of International Law* (1998), 9(2), pp. 355–67.
13. For Bobbio, the term 'legal-political' means a recognition of the interdependence between legal and political theory to address specific issues. For him, it is an abortive exercise to set law up against politics, or politics against law.
14. N. Bobbio, 'Congedo', in L. Bonanate and M. Bovero (eds), *Per una teoria generale della politica: scritti dedicati a Norberto Bobbio* [*A General Theory of Politics: Essays in Honour of Norberto Bobbio*] (Florence, Passigli 1986), pp. 241–53.
15. 'Un carteggio tra Norberto Bobbio e Perry Anderson' ['An exchange between Norberto Bobbio and Perry Anderson'], *Teoria politica* (1989), 5(2), p. 295.
16. 'L'utopia capovolta' ['The upturned utopia'], *La Stampa* (1989), 9 June.
17. 'The upturned utopia', *New Left Review* (1989), 177, pp. 37–9.
18. 'My admiration for Enlightenment authors', he avers, 'has taught me to guard myself against the temptation of fanaticism': 'Carl Schmitt, Norberto Bobbio', *Diritto e Cultura* (1995), January–June, 1, pp. 49–80.
19. 'Scienza del diritto e analisi del linguaggio', *Rivista trimestrale di diritto e procedura civile* (1950), IV(2), June, pp. 342–67.
20. 'Riflessioni autobiografiche', *Nuova Antologia* (1993), 2185, January–March, pp. 49–50.
21. 'At the beginning of history', *New Left Review* (1998), 231, September–October, p. 83.
22. Kant uses the term in 'The contest of faculties' (p. 178) and 'Idea for a universal history with a cosmopolitan purpose' (p. 50) in H. Reiss, *Kant's Political Writings* (Cambridge, Cambridge University Press 1977).
23. 'Democracy and the international system', in D. Archibugi and D. Held (eds), *Cosmopolitan Democracy: An Agenda for a New World Order* (Cambridge, Polity Press 1995), pp. 17–41.

24. Hans Jonas, *Mortality and Morality: A Search for the Good after Auschwitz* (Evanston IL, Northwestern University Press 1996).
25. Umberto Eco, 'A rose by any other name', *Convivio* (1995), 1(1), p. 42, and originally in *Guardian Weekly* (1994), 16 January, p. 20.
26. These interviews were conducted throughout the 1990s during periods of extended field work based at the University of Turin. I regularly clarify points with him by telephone.
27. Some interpretative comments of mine on Bobbio's recently translated books are found in: 'Norberto Bobbio's political thought', *Times Literary Supplement* (1994), 5 August, 13; 'The age of rights', *Times Higher Educational Supplement* (1997), 3 January; and 'Book Review: Norberto Bobbio, *Ideological Profile of Twentieth Century Italy; The Age of Rights; Left and Right*', *Theory and Society* (1998), 27(3), pp. 411–17. My translations of Bobbio include 'Revolution between movement and change', *Thesis Eleven* (1997), 48, February, pp. 113–29, originally as N. Bobbio, 'La rivoluzione tra movimento e mutamento', *Teoria politica* (1989), V(2–3), pp. 3–21; 'The closed and open society [1946]', *Australian Journal of Politics & History* (1996), 42(1), pp. 84–9, originally as N. Bobbio, 'Società chiusa, e società aperta', *Il Ponte* (1946), pp. 1039–46. Bobbio's *Tra due repubbliche – Alle origini della democrazia italiana* (Rome, Donzelli 1996) is analysed in two articles: 'Norberto Bobbio and the two republics. I. The responsible citizen', *Convivio* (1997), 3(2), pp. 134–44; and 'Norberto Bobbio and the two republics. II. The republic for all citizens', *Convivio* (1998), 4(1), pp. 45–57. A comprehensive interpretative text, *Norberto Bobbio: Law and Cosmopolitical Democracy*, written as the goal of my ARC Postdoctoral Fellowship held during 1998–2000, is forthcoming.

Introduction

In the final pages of *Dialogo su una vita di studi* my interlocutor, Pietro Polito, invited me to discuss the 1994 edition of *Elogio della mitezza* [*In Praise of Meekness*], which at the time I termed 'self-indulgent'. I presented it as a booklet that enables one to see, beside and beyond the legal and political philosopher, the moral philosopher as well.[1] In recent years, having experienced the effects of old age, I became absorbed and preoccupied with the question of evil in the world and throughout history. Hence, I loosened my links with the sphere of politics. It is not accidental, but perhaps premonitory, that some years ago, when invited to participate in a series of seminars on the virtues, I chose 'meekness'. I included it among the weak virtues, as opposed to the strong virtues of a state leader, and defined it as 'the least political virtue'.

Recently, a benevolent reader and critic used examples from my recent books, *De Senectute* (1996) and *Autobiografia* (1997), to observe how over time I increasingly provided an 'ethical dimension' to my writings. This arose from the fact that I elevated 'moral forces' that prevent institutions from degenerating, and asserted that 'even more than good laws, the basis of a good republic rests on the virtue of its citizens'.[2] To be honest, the common idea that democracy needs democratically virtuous citizens is an old notion of mine. I have never forgotten Croce's warning that invites us to contrast politics with 'non-political force with which good politics must always reckon'.[3]

However, my definition of meekness as a non-political virtue was not well received by my old and dear friend Giuliano Pontara, the major Italian scholar of Gandhi, and a passionate and erudite theorist of nonviolence. His response appeared in the same journal that published my essay. After some pertinent observations about my theoretical premises, and about my consideration of meekness as a passive virtue, he rejected my identification of meekness with nonviolence. From this, in his view, one could logically deduce the negation by nonviolence of any political value, and therefore it would be impossible to differentiate passive nonviolence inherent in traditional pacifists from active nonviolence, as theorized and practised by Gandhi, and which is a highly political virtue.

According to Pontara:

Nonviolence has a role in politics, which is as effective as were Gandhi's presence and the role he played in politics. But it is within politics in an altogether special way, and in this consists the real novelty and currency of the Gandhian message. Because he is meek, a nonviolent person does not engage in conflictual relations with others aiming to contest, destroy or defeat. He is not vindictive, he does not bear grudges, he does not hold resentment or hate towards anyone, and he is not power-hungry. He is certainly never the first to start a quarrel, but he is not afraid to engage in a conflict. Rather, he is not fearful of bringing latent conflicts to the surface, nor is he frightened of struggle. But, in the same way as he rejects violence [...], he also rejects the logic of power according to which there is always the need for a winner and a loser. Furthermore, he considers conflicts in such a way that the solution will never be zero-sum, but rather a solution in which all sides profit by it, and hence is accepted by all. To that end, he engages in the struggle using methods that do not threaten his opponent's vital interests. These solicit his good qualities, as well as appealing to the more open and sensitive groups within the opposite side. He uses methods of struggle that tend to humanize rather than de-humanize his opponent [...]. Nonviolence, therefore, is the channel through which meekness becomes strength, and works differently from that of violence. A nonviolent person rejects violence, but without having to withdraw from politics due to this. By his actions he disproves the definition of politics as being the exclusive domain of the fox and the lion.[4]

I responded briefly and, I acknowledge, somewhat irritatedly, reducing our disagreement to a question of words on the meaning of 'politics'. My intended meaning was manifestly the Machiavellian sense, although I was well acquainted with Gandhi's nonviolent theory and practice, and of course Pontara knew this. In the friendly reply that concluded our dialogue, Pontara was keen to convey to me that his anxiety derived from the fact that by not taking into account the distinction between active nonviolence and passive nonviolence, I had been led to a somewhat too simplistic identification of meekness with nonviolence. I fully understood. This reinforces the common prejudice that identifies politics with violence, and denies that political action can be effected by nonviolent means.

Enrico Peyretti's comment is not much different. Taking as a point of departure the evangelical maxim 'Blessed are the meek for they will inherit the earth' (Matthew V:5), he posed the question: 'Which of the two human types, the powerful or the meek, will actually govern the earth? Who will manage, preserve and nurture it, so that it can contextualize and embody history, and represent the long course of humanity?' Adhering to Capitini's conviction, he describes himself as 'someone persuaded by nonviolence', and observes that in effect politics generally banishes meekness. Nevertheless, he asks whether there may be 'another kind of politics' beyond that which 'considers the attainment of power by any means as its principal criterion, and yet is incapable of guaranteeing stable peace, which is the prime aim of politics'. He concludes by questioning the 'amoral' theory of politics that shuns meekness.[5]

There were others who gave different opinions. Among various letters received there is one by a group of secondary school students. Their teacher read them some pages of my *Elogio*, which they heard about from Arturo Colombo's review in *Corriere della Sera* (1995), 1 March, 'Arroganti e prepotenti, la mitezza vi seppellirà' ['Meekness will bury the arrogant and the domineering']. They were persuaded that it was wrong for some people to lead others to believe that 'meekness is weakness'. I am grateful to these students, their teacher, and their inspirer for recognizing that meekness, as I described it, is indeed a weak virtue, but it is not the virtue of the weak. I had clearly stated that meekness was not to be confused with either submissiveness or docility.

The two essays in part I address the assertion that a moral theory of politics eschews meekness. Once again, this raises the old and perennial question of the relation between morals and politics. When Peyretti states that 'violent politics, the kind that ostracize politics, are not politics',[6] he regards the problem as solved, by including the conformity of political action with moral principles in the definition of politics, which I would not hesitate to consider persuasive. It is well known that in the history of political thought we find two concepts of politics alongside each other and in mutual opposition, the Aristotelian and the Christian. According to these, 'political action' means any action aimed at either the wellbeing of the city or the common good. Realist politics becomes established through Machiavelli, Guicciardini, and theorists of the reason of state, according to which the sphere of politics is autonomous with respect to that of morals. Moreover, the action of a state leader cannot be judged on the basis of rules that regulate, and by which the action of an ordinary person is judged.[7] The question was regarded as solved by the prevailing reason of state theory, especially in Italian culture, from Benedetto Croce to Rodolfo De Mattei to Luigi Firpo, by maintaining, if not the morality, the amorality of politics, albeit leaving out of consideration reasons that justify such amorality. However, more recently the question has been reposed by the movement for the so-called 'rehabilitation of practical philosophy' that goes back to Aristotle. In Italian culture this is addressed by Maurizio Viroli, who re-examines this tradition by tracing it in the history of Italian medieval political thought. In particular he highlights the 'transformation of political language', in the transition from the classical conception of politics to reason of state theory.[8]

In my view, the two concepts of politics cannot be separated, either analytically or historically. The positive and negative visions of politics pursue and oppose each other in every age. The distinction between good and bad government, which Viroli captures in the contrast between the art of government and the science of the state, is a classical topos in political thought. It has its origins in the Aristotelian distinction between pure and corrupt forms of government. According to this distinction, the good forms are those of a ruler whose use of power is aimed at the common good, and the bad forms are those of the ruler who uses power for self-interest. This distinction is transmitted from age to age, so that we find it even in the distinction between a good and bad reason of state, by those same authors who rejected the classical theory of politics. Moreover, the distinguished historian Gerhard Ritter wrote his absorbing book *The Corrupting Influence of Power* precisely on the period when the big turning point occurred.[9] There it is maintained that the two antagonistic currents of power, the realistic by Machiavelli and the utopian by Thomas More, diverge from the beginning of the sixteenth century and persist right up to the present.

Likewise, without historical precedents, when considering reason of state theory, I am uncertain which can be viewed as the wicked form of politics. The core of this theory rests entirely on the famous maxim that originates with Cicero, *salus rei publicae suprema lex* [the highest law is the security of the state]. In effect, Machiavelli, the very same theorist who, according to Viroli, is excluded from reason of state theory, appropriates it in the famous passage of the *Discourses* III.41 (rather than in the notorious *The Prince*). There he states that when the safety of the country is at risk, 'it is good to defend one's country in whatever way it be done, whether it entail ignominy or glory'.

In any event, among the various interpretations of the dissociation between ethics and politics, Viroli did not miss the one advanced by Scipione Ammirato, according to which it is right 'to violate ordinary laws out of respect for public benefit'. This concerns a general principle of law and ethics that accepts derogation of a law in exceptional cases.[10]

Among these, the predominant and most frequently invoked is the state of necessity, a cause of justification that, as everyone knows, is also valid for single individuals. Felix Oppenheim more recently wrote a book where he maintains that the state-as-actor model is justified. Hence, when it becomes necessary to defend the national interest, the state cannot be subjected to moral judgement.[11] What is the national interest other than the *salus rei publicae* of the Ancients?

The two essays in part II on the nature of prejudice and on racism are closely connected. Not only is prejudice the root of racism, but prejudice reinforces it. It is difficult to think of an individual motivated by a strong aversion towards an individual of another race who does not try to justify it by resorting to judgements unsupported by any actual proof. There is a need, however, to differentiate between racism as behaviour, or as habitual attitude, non-reflexive and emotional, and racism as a theory that claims to be scientific, ideologically inspired and directed. In turn, racism as ideology must be distinguished from the scientific study of human races, which, even when it is able to establish the existence of different human groups that can rightly be called 'races', does not provide any support for racist ideology. This not only maintains that different races exist, and that there are superior and inferior races, but also claims that the superior race as such has the right to dominate the inferior. Even the relationship between parents and children, or teachers and students, is in fact, and nearly always also in law, a relationship between a superior and a subordinate. But it is a relationship in which the superior, instead of claiming the right to dominate those who are inferior, takes on the duty to help, support, and redeem them from their subordination. Since ancient times, as is made clear in some famous pages by Aristotle, the power of a superior over the subordinate assumes two quite different forms. These are the power of a father over his children that is exercised for their benefit, and the power of the master over the slaves that is exercised in favour of the master. From these two different types of power of the superior and the subordinate within the familial group emerge two quite different forms of authoritarian state. The first is the paternalistic, or, to use an expression derived from the Old Testament rather than the classical tradition, the patriarchal. The other is a despotic government, where the holder of power, or rule, treats his subjects likes slaves. It can be deduced from the foregoing that a person can quite well be racist without accepting the scientific or pseudo-scientific theory of the division of humanity into races. Similarly, one can be a polygenist without being racist, that is, maintain that human groups did not emerge from the same root. Conversely, by rejecting polygenism one can be racist.

Since humans are as much the same as they are different, similar because unlike other animals they can speak, and different because they speak in different languages, it is as false to generalize that they are all the same as it is to say that they are all different. Two contrasting immigration policies derive from these false generalizations, respectively. At one extreme there is assimilation, effected through the gradual acquisition of citizenship rights, first individual, then civil and political, and finally social. Assimilation requires that those who enter a country must gradually identify with its inhabitants, accept its rules, customs, language, and mentality, in order to become something different from what they were. Thus they lose their identity, which is what constitutes their 'difference'. At the other extreme, in recent years, and precisely as a reaction to the assimilation policy, there has been a stronger demand for respect of differences. This should allow the claimant of difference the widest possible preservation of the differences that make the difference. These include customs, language, and consequently the right to worship, to attend a particular school, and to observe chosen holy days, and even the right to a traditional mode of dress (consider, for example, the recent debate on the use of the chador by Muslim female students in French schools).

In summary, these two policies are representative of two forms of prejudice, or in other words, of an undisputed belief that is accepted as absolute in that 'Humans are all the same, irrespective of any difference.' But if they are all the same, why differentiate between them? If they are all different, why make them all the same?

Today, the clash between these two extreme solutions is more alive than ever. But precisely because they are extreme solutions, they are perhaps both incorrect. This is because, against the two contrasting prejudices, humans are as much the same as they are different. Since, according to the liberal vision of coexistence, there are fundamental rights of individuals that must be recognized by the state, no one can be so egalitarian as not to recognize the right to religious diversity. This implies the right of everyone to worship their own God, or not to worship at all. Equally, no one can differentiate so much as not to recognize the sameness of others irrespective of their origins, even the most distant. This applies not only spatially, but also culturally with respect to human rights. The first of these are individual rights that come before citizenship rights, and are in fact their premise.

Within democratic civilization, one must not be afraid to state that the solution to the problem rests in the reconciliation of the two opposing needs, each with its own reason. This can occur once the prejudices that support them are recognized, namely that each person is the same as another, and each person is different from another.

The same factors that forced some nations, Italy among them, to confront the problem of new immigration flows which generate wicked and dangerous racist attitudes and behaviours have reopened and revived the old theme of tolerance on a theoretical basis. When one speaks of tolerance in its predominant historical meaning, as expressed in my essay 'Tolerance and truth' included here, the problem of the coexistence of different beliefs, the religious followed by the political, is addressed. Today, the principle of tolerance is extended to the question of coexistence with ethnic, linguistic, and racial minorities, more generally with those considered 'different', such as homosexuals, the mentally ill, or the handicapped. The questions to which these two ways of understanding and practising tolerance refer are not the same. The question of tolerance of different beliefs or opinions that requires consideration of both the theoretical and above all the practical compatibility of truths, even those that are opposed, is one thing. It is another to have to consider the question of tolerance with respect to those who are different for physical or social reasons, which brings to the fore the theme of prejudice and its consequent discrimination. The reasons that can be advanced in support of tolerance in the first meaning are not the same as those that support it in the other meaning. Likewise, the reasons for the two forms of intolerance are also different. The first derives from the conviction of possessing truth, whereas the other, as stated, is usually based on a prejudice. It is also true that the conviction of possessing truth can be false, and thus can take the form of prejudice. But this is a prejudice that is fought in a completely different way. One cannot place on the same level arguments advanced to convince the faithful of a particular church, or followers of a political party, to coexist with other faiths or with other parties, as arguments to persuade a white person to coexist peacefully with a black. The fundamental question that advocates of religious or political tolerance have always asked themselves can be formulated as follows: 'How can two opposing truths be theoretically and practically compatible?' A supporter of tolerance for those who are different asks this further question: 'How can one demonstrate that certain intolerances of a minority of persons who are different derive from deep-rooted prejudices, from irrational, or simply emotional, forms of judging humans and events?' The best proof of this difference rests in the fact that in the second case, the usual term that designates what must be fought is not intolerance but discrimination.

In the two essays included in part III, 'Truth and liberty' and 'Tolerance and truth', which are closely connected, tolerance is discussed not so much from the viewpoint of its legal justification, but rather from its moral justification. The aim is to defend tolerance from the charge of being the expression of relativist morals, and of moral indifferentism or scepticism.

The subject has been widely discussed in recent years, prompted by an article where Ernesto Galli della Loggia raises certain issues. Through some persuasive arguments that, in my view, should be taken seriously, he admonishes 'progressive liberal secularism' for its 'annoying self-importance'.

He argues that by secularism professing to defend itself from the charge of delegitimizing the question of values that drive our society resulted in the renewal of religious ethics.[12] I became personally involved by writing 'In praise of tolerance', where I took up both the subject of the relation between tolerance and truth, and reasons why one can be tolerant without being sceptical. I remarked that I shared Galli della Loggia's disapproval when what is meant by tolerance is not 'the opposite of intolerance but rather moral rigour. That is, firmness in maintaining one's ideas, and fair severity in judgement.' But I also mentioned the renewal, especially in the English-speaking world, of studies in rational ethics, which strangely enough were not raised in the article, or in the ensuing debate.

Recently, the subject of the weakness, fragility, or inconsistency of lay ethics compared with Catholic ethics was again raised, in more or less similar terms, by Giuliano Amato in an interview in *Il Mondo*, which was taken up by *La Stampa* on 30 August 1997. Rejecting the prevalence of the unfettered market, Amato voiced his admiration for the community of St Egidio and its charitable work. Concerned, and with some dismay, he asked himself why 'lay persons are incapable of translating their ethical values into organized action'. He also admitted that, personally, he was living a contradiction that created doubt for which he could find no solution.[13]

Gianni Vattimo's stern critique also appeared in that newspaper. He concluded, notwithstanding the value of liberty for both lay persons and Catholics, with praise for the open society and the assertion that Popper's time (the author most acknowledged for his authoritative support of lay ethics) is anything but over. Provided lay persons do not renounce their responsibility, his time is yet to come. As Vattimo remarks: 'Realization of the minimal conditions of liberty (economic and spiritual) can make programmes work much more than do laments over lost values.'[14]

In the final two essays, 'For and against lay ethics' and 'The gods that failed', I openly confront two issues. In the first, I address the fundamental question that is implied in the preceding pages. This concerns relations between lay ethics and religious ethics with regard to compatibility or incompatibility, and reciprocal indifference or reciprocal amalgamation, depending on the different perspectives. In the other, the question of Evil is the principal subject on the basis of which, in my view, one can assess the difference and the difficulty in the dialogue between lay persons and the religious.

In effect, instead of speaking about lay ethics, there is a need to consider a lay vision of the world and of history, as distinct from a religious vision. One can also speak in everyday language about the distinction between a sacred and a profane conception, or, in the currently preferred expression, a deconsecrated conception of the world and of history that originated with the modern age, and, following Weber, is termed the period of 'disenchantment'. Alongside profane history, for a Christian there is a sacred history, whose only undisputed guide is the church, or the different churches, which derive their inspiration from the Holy Scriptures. For a lay person, there is only one history, and it is the one we live, with our unresolved doubts and unanswered questions. For this history, the only guide is our anything but infallible reason that draws data from experience upon which to reflect. This is the history with no other preceding or superseding history. Our history is merely an imperfect prefiguration, an unfaithful or even a deceptive reflection. The vision of a lay person lacks the dimension of hope in a final deliverance, redemption, palingenesis, or, simply stated, in salvation. There is no place for salvation in a vision of the world that does not include the original sin that, once and for all, stained the whole of humanity from its centuries-old origins. For lay persons, history does not unfold according to a predetermined course, already traced from the beginning, between original sin and final redemption. Rather, it is a history of events whose concatenation of causes can probably, though not always, be sought, but seldom is the attribution of faults possible. It is a history for which it is useless to try to find an ultimate meaning because this does not exist, or at least until now it has not been so clearly revealed as to compel agreement. Where is the sense in the dreadful cyclone that some years ago devastated Bangladesh, and decimated its population, or, to recall an earlier event, the earthquake in Messina? This occurred precisely at the beginning of the tragic twentieth century, destroying an entire city, famous in the history of the West, and killing a large number of its inhabitants. I am aware that asking these kinds of question can cause dismay, and can also be the subject of facile accusations by believers for whom 'not a leaf stirs unless God wills it'. Moreover, for them everything must have a meaning, including the loss of life caused by a flood or an earthquake. But a lay person cannot renounce expressing his doubts about his limited and tormented humanity, or cease to pose questions continually through which he seeks to find a way out of the darkness that surrounds him, without forsaking the awareness he has gradually acquired from reflecting on life and death. For a man of reason it makes no sense, if you will excuse my quibble, to question the meaning in an event such as a flood, or an earthquake, which is unforeseeable, unexpected, and distressing not only for its consequences but also for its unintelligibility.

The contrast between the man of reason and the man of faith is, in my view, difficult to remedy. I am, however, receptive to the opinions of those who believe otherwise. That contrast is revealed with all its dramatic implications in the discussion on the subject of Evil, contained in the final essay and appendix, where I reply to two authoritative interlocutors.[15]

Above all, my aim was to differentiate, more clearly than is usually done, between active evil, or wickedness, and passive evil, or, suffering, or, stated differently, between inflicted evil and endured evil. Still, in a 1982 book by Albert Görres and Karl Rahner,[16] the problem is introduced by using the old and absolutely incongruous distinction between moral evil and physical evil. I say 'incongruous' because it considers the evils as two types of the same kind. Thus it obfuscates the need to keep the two problems completely separate, since their connection is seen only through a vision of human history and the universe where suffering, or physical evil, would be the direct or indirect consequence of moral evil. This is the way it is usually presented in devotional religious texts, where the sick person is also a sinner, and deliverance from evil and from illness coincide.[17] It is a vision of history and of the universe that leaves completely unexplained the suffering derived from natural disasters and the cruelty that predominates in the animal world. With the latter, while one can quite rightly speak of physical evil, it makes no sense to speak about moral evil. The greater part of the suffering experienced by human beings in this vale of tears, out of which the plea 'it would have been better not to be born' often emerges, has nothing to do with someone's guilt. Nor is it to do with one's own, or even with evil understood as a wicked deed. While inflicted evil can be explained mythically by original sin, endured evil, often without guilt, cannot.

In a lay vision of life there is no absolute Evil. Instead, there are many forms of evil. More precisely, these consist of many different events that fall within an all-inclusive category of Evil, too general to be pragmatically useful, and which analytically should be quite distinct. Any reflection on evil should begin with the phenomenology of the different forms of evil and 'certain boundary situations', as undertaken by Paul Ricoeur, albeit in a way that, in my view, is not altogether satisfactory.[18]

Yet, at the heart of this great dichotomy, how many other distinctions should be advanced before confronting the problem of the causes and remedies? Not all inflicted evil can be regarded as falling within the category of absolute Evil, or of evil defined as absolute solely because one is unable to find a possible explanation for it, with the ever-present example in current debates being Auschwitz. There are endless gradations in the dimension of an evil deed, quite well known to moral theologians and jurists, and on which it is inappropriate to elaborate here. While both premeditated and unintentional murder fall within the category of inflicted evil, they cannot be treated in the same way. Even inside the other dimension of evil, that of suffering, the difference between physical and psychological suffering, and between psychological and moral suffering, is obvious. One cannot compare a toothache with the pain due to the loss of a loved one, or with the regret for an act we have committed in breaking a rule or causing harm to others. The difference becomes considerable when one reflects on the possible remedies for either one or the other source of suffering. Physical suffering can be reduced, or even eliminated, through medication. One need only reflect on the importance of anaesthesia in aiding the development of surgery. Today, even those who adopt a religious point of view do not oppose the use of these remedies.

The situation that concerns psychological or moral suffering, however, is quite different. When that suffering entails the death of a loved one, either there is no remedy, or the only possible one is the natural and relentless passage of time. There is also no easy remedy for suffering from the evil one has committed, which includes regret. There is no remedy for this except expiation, that is, through self-punishment, or by forgiveness, which is an act of goodwill by the injured party.

These and other observations that could be made are the ABC of any analysis of the problem of evil that proposes to address the issue, leaving out of consideration the existence of God. At this point, the difficulty is quite clear, even in the mind of those who consider the problem from a religious viewpoint, so that especially in recent times, attempts have been made at more satisfactory solutions than the traditional, from which the different theodicies originated. A possible solution, which I will only mention, has been sought in redefining the concept of God in such a way as to render the existence of God compatible with that of Evil.[19]

The solution of the insoluble mystery of Evil within the problem of all the other evils that afflict humans is not an act of rationalist arrogance. On the contrary, it is, quite modestly, the first condition that from time to time enables a man of reason, or a scientist, albeit conscious of his limitations, to find some effective remedy that will make evil more endurable.

Norberto Bobbio

Notes

1. N. Bobbio and P. Polito, 'Dialogo su una vita di studi' ['Dialogue on a Lifetime of Research'], *Nuova Antologia* (1996), 131, 577 (2200), October–December, p. 60.
2. C. Ocone, 'Qual è il vero Bobbio?' ['Which is the real Bobbio'], *Critica liberale* (1997), IV (35) November, p. 143. Ocone refers to a statement in my *Autobiografia*, A. Papuzzi (ed.) (Rome/Bari, Laterza 1997), p. 257.
3. B. Croce, *Indagini su Hegel e schiarimenti filosofici* [*On Hegel: An Inquiry and Philosophical Explanations*] (Rome/Bari, Laterza 1952), pp. 159–60.
4. Pontara's essay, 'Il mite e il nonviolento. Su un saggio di Norberto Bobbio' ['The meek and nonviolent person. On an essay by Norberto Bobbio'] was first published, followed by my reply, in *Linea d'ombra* (1994) 93, March, pp. 67–70. Pontara's response, 'Sulla nonviolenza. Risposta a Bobbio' ['On nonviolence. An answer to Bobbio'], was published in the same journal, (1994) 94, May–June, pp. 71–3. Pontara's essay and my reply, together with his response, were included in the first edition of this book (Rome, Linea d'ombra Edizioni 1994), pp. 33–41. More recently, Pontara republished his intervention under the title 'Virtù, mitezza e nonviolenza' ['Virtue, meekness and nonviolence'] in *Guerre, disobbedienza civile, nonviolenza* [*Wars, Civil Disobedience, Nonviolence*] (Turin, Edizioni Gruppo Abele 1996), pp. 83–95. With reference to my reply and Pontara's response, see below.
5. E. Peyretti, 'Elogio della mitezza esiliata. Note sugli scritti morali di Norberto Bobbio', ['In praise of banished meekness. Notes on Norberto Bobbio's moral writings'], *Il Foglio* (1995), XXV (2), February, p. 3. Peyretti is editor of the small monthly journal *Il Foglio*, of which I am an assiduous reader (and which is not to be confused with Giuliano Ferrara's daily of the same name).
6. Ibid.
7. It is so well known that in the entry 'Politik' [*Politics*] in *Geschichtliche Grundbegriffe* (Stuttgart, Ernst Klett Verlag 1975) the author, Volker Sellin, devotes a section to the 'foundations of the concept of politics in the modern age, the Aristotelian heritage, and Machiavelli's notion of power'. See the

Italian edition *Politica*, with a preface by L. Ornaghi (Venezia, Marsilio 1993), pp. 49–57.

8. M. Viroli, *Dalla politica alla ragion di stato: La scienza del governo tra XIII e XVIII secolo* [*From Politics to Reason of State The Science of Government during the XIIIth and XVIIIth Centuries*] (Rome, Donzelli 1994). The subject of reason of state has in recent years undergone significant development in research and debates among historians, not only Italian, of political thought. The following are some references: A. E. Baldini (ed.), *Botero e la ragion di stato* [*Botero and the Reason of State*], Atti del Convegno in memoria di L. Firpo, 8–10 March 1990, (Florence, Leo S. Olschki 1992); G. Borrelli, *Ragion di stato e Leviatano: Conservazione e scambio alle origini della modernità politica* [*Reason of State and Leviathan: Preservation and Exchange at the Origins of Political Modernity*] (Bologna, Il Mulino 1993); special issue of *Trimestre* (1993) (University of Teramo) devoted to Rodolfo De Mattei, XXVI(2–3); A. E. Baldini (ed.), *Aristotelismo e ragion di stato* [*Aristotelian Theory and Reason of State*], Atti del Convegno internazionale, 11–13 February 1993, (Florence, Olschki 1995); G. Borrelli (ed.), *Ragion di stato: L'arte italiana della prudenza politica* [*Reason of State: The Italian Art of Political Prudence*] (Naples, Mostra bibliografica, Istituto italiano per gli studi filosofici 1994); Yves Charles Zarka (ed.), *Raison et déraison d'Etat: Théoriciens et théories de la raison d'Etat aux XVI et XVII siécle* [*Reason of State and State Irrationality in the XVI and XVIII Centuries*] (Paris, Presses Universitaires de France 1994). In 1993 the *Archivio della Ragion di Stato* [*Archives of Reason of State*], ed. *G. Borrelli*, began publication of original articles, news, and bibliographies.

9. G. Ritter, *The Corrupting Influence of Power* (Tower Bridge, Hadleigh 1952), and 'The fault of mass democracy', in J. L. Snell (ed.), *The Nazi Revolution: Germany's Guilt or Germany's Fate* (Boston, Heath 1959), pp. 76–84.

10. Viroli, *Dalla politica alla ragion di stato*, pp. 179–80.

11. F. E. Oppenheim, *The Place of Morality in Foreign Policy* (Lexington, Heath 1991), especially ch. 1.

12. E. Galli della Loggia, 'Mea culpa di un laico' ['Mea culpa of a lay person'] *La Stampa* (1998), 28 September. This article generated a debate on lay culture with the first contribution by S.Quinzio, 'Gli antichi valori perduti' ['The old values lost'] *La Stampa* (1988), 29 September. This was followed by A. Galante Garrone, 'Non ha tramonto la regola della

libertà' ['The rule of liberty never wanes'], *La Stampa* (1988), 30 September; then P.Bonetti, 'Laico é chi non concede indebiti privilegi' ['A lay person is someone who does not yield to undue privileges'], *La Stampa* (1988), 1 October; D. Cofrancesco, 'È il prezzo della libertà' ['It is the price of liberty'], *Il Secolo XIX* (1998), 5 October; G.Vattimo, 'Per essere davvero individui' ['To be truly individuals'], *La Stampa* (1988), 6 October; U. Scarpelli, 'Laicismo e morale' (Laicism and morals), *Il Sole-24 ore* (1988) 7 October. On 9 October 1988 my reply, 'Lode della tolleranza' ['In praise of tolerance'], appeared in *La Stampa*, and on 12 October the debate was concluded with an article by Galli della Loggia, 'Ansie senza risposta' ['Unanswered anxieties'], where he laments the restrictive conception of liberalism as method that rests upon two values which have increasingly revealed their insufficiency in the face of contemporary problems, such as individualism and rationalism. This resulted in producing a platform for these discussions of a moral nature, and therefore assigning the authority to transmit values only to the traditional powers such as the churches. A sequel to the debate, with broad participation, occurred on 30 October in *L'Espresso* through the article 'Laici addio?' ['Farewell to lay persons?'], begun by F. Adornato, who besides Galli della Loggia also interviews E. Scalfari and L. Colletti. On 30 October 1988 an article by G. Pasquarelli, 'Metamorfosi della cultura laica' ['The metamorphosis of lay culture'] appeared in *Il tempo*, where lay culture is accused of retreating in itself, of lacking a soul, and of encouraging contemporary immoralism.

13. G. Amato, 'Etica: la forza del papa' ['Ethics: the pope's strength'], an interview with A. Satta, *La Stampa* (1997), 30 August.

14. G. Vattimo, 'Le paure dei laici' ['The fears of lay persons'] *La Stampa* (1997), 30 August.

15. My no less authoritative and friendly interlocutors are Enrico Peyretti, 'Sul male regnante, sulla mitezza esiliata' ['On ruling evil and banished meekness'], *Il Foglio* (1995), XXV(1), January, pp. 1–2; Vittorio Possenti, 'Dio e il male' ['God and evil'], in Vittorio Possenti, *Dio e il male* [*God and Evil*] (Turin, SEI 1995).

16. A. Görres and K. Rahner, *Il male: Le risposte della psicoterapia e del cristianesimo* [*Evil. Answers from Psychotherapy and Christianity*] (Turin, Edizioni Paoline 1987).

17. U. Bonanate, *Nascita di una religione: Le origini del cristiane-simo* [*The Birth of a Religion: The Origins of Christianity*] (Turin, Bollati Boringhieri 1994) p. 21.

18. P. Ricoeur, 'Evil, a challenge to philosophy and theology', in his *Figuring the Sacred: Religion, Narrative, and Imagination*, ed. M. I. Wallace, tr. D. Pellauer (Minneapolis, Fortress 1995), pp. 249–61.

19. With regard to Pareyson's philosophy of evil, which would deserve a deeper analysis, see V. Possenti, *Dio e il male* [*God and Evil*] (Turin, SEI 1995), p. 11ff. On the history of the problem of evil from Leibniz onwards, refer to the recent work by E.Spedicato, *La strana creatura del caos: Idee e figure del male nel pensiero della modernità* [*The Strange Creature of Chaos: Ideas and Images of Evil in the Theory of Modernity*] (Rome, Donzelli 1997).

In Praise of Meekness

Among the ancients, ethics were largely resolved through the treatment of virtues. Suffice it to recall Aristotle's *Nicomachean Ethics*, which was for centuries a prescribed text. In our times such a treatment has almost disappeared. Today, moral philosophers debate on both analytical and propositional levels about values and choices and their greater or lesser rationality. They also argue over rules or norms and, consequently, over rights and duties. One of the last significant writings devoted to the classic subject of virtue was the second part of Kant's *Metaphysics of Morals*, titled 'The theory of virtue'. The first part deals with the 'Theory of law'. Kant's ethics, however, are principally ethics of duty, and more specifically of inward as distinguished from outward duty, which is the concern of legal theory. In that writing virtue is defined as the willpower necessary to fulfil one's duty, and as the moral strength humans need to resist those defects that prevent or hinder the accomplishment of duty. Kant's theory of virtue is an integral part of the ethics of duty and, as is explicitly and repeatedly maintained, has nothing to do with Aristotelian ethics.

Throughout the centuries when European philosophy was prominent, the traditional subject of virtues and, correspondingly, of vices became the subject of treatises on the passions. Representative of these are Descartes's *Passions of the Soul*, the section titled 'The origins of natural affections', Spinoza's *Ethics*, and the introductory chapters of Hobbes's *Elements of Natural Law and Politics* and *Leviathan*. The theory of ethics, on the other hand, found and for some centuries maintained its place within natural law theory. In that context the perspective of (moral, legal, and ethical) laws or norms prevailed within the analysis of the elements of morals. The solution of ethics therefore is articulated through the theory of duties and of rights, respectively. In Pufendorf's classic and better-known treatise, *De jure naturae et gentium*, the subject of virtues in the traditional sense receives little attention in the chapter on human will.

The analysis of virtues preserved its natural expression in the writings of moralists, all but forgotten today. Rather, in affluent societies a moralist is generally considered a killjoy, a spoilsport, or someone unable to enjoy life. A moralist has become synonymous with a moaner, a somewhat ridiculous pedagogue who can be ignored, someone who preaches to the wind, or criticizes customs. In short, a moralist is as boring as, fortunately, he is innocuous. If one wishes to silence a citizen who is still capable of protesting or becoming indignant, one need simply call him a moralist, and he is done for. In recent years we have had many occasions to observe that whenever anyone criticizes general corruption, or the abuse of either economic or political power, he is forced to state defensively: 'I am not doing this because I am a moralist.' As if to say he did not want anything to do with those sorts of people, since they are generally held in such low esteem.

When I gave my address on 'meekness', Alasdair MacIntyre's provocative book, *After Virtue: A Study in Moral Theory*, had not been published yet or, at least, I was not aware of it. It is now well known, since it was translated into Italian in 1988.[1] This work is an attempt to reinstate the subject of virtue, which was unjustly and damagingly discarded, to its honourable place and re-present it to readers of today. Thus it might resume its interrupted journey that began with Aristotle. MacIntyre's thought proceeds through a continuous argument that, in my view, does not always appear genuine, or very original, against several questions. Among these he addresses emotivism, the distinction between facts and values, and individualism, which he terms 'bureaucratic'. With respect to all the ills of the modern world, he regards the Enlightenment as principally responsible through the prevailing of ethical rationalism that inevitably converged into nihilism. This certainly is not the place to engage in a critical analysis of this book, since for my purpose here, it confirms the neglect into which the theory of virtue had lapsed. MacIntyre proposes his book as a work against the trend, as a return to tradition, and as a challenge to 'the distinctively modern and modernizing world' (p. x). One of his preferred targets is legal ethics. In his view, the ethics of virtue stand in opposition to legal ethics, which have gradually prevailed in modern and contemporary ethics. Legal ethics constitute the ethics of rights and duties.

I have always held a certain hesitation in accepting such drastic contrasts because they encourage unilateral attitudes towards subjects that are as elusive as the philosophical, where truth is never summarily, definitively, and indisputably on either one or the other side. I similarly hesitate with respect to a possible interpretation of history as a huge container filled randomly with all sorts of things, which makes it nearly always dangerous and rather inconclusive to isolate one item among the many.

The question of whether traditional ethics were prevalently the ethics of virtues opposed to the ethics of rules (or more exactly, legal ethics) is quite debatable. It would require forgetting *The Laws*, one of Plato's great works. In Aristotle's *Nicomachean Ethics*, one aspect of the virtue of justice is the custom of obeying the laws. The subject of virtue and the subject of laws are continually interwoven, even in the ethics of the ancients. At the basis of our moral tradition, and as the foundation of our civic education, there are both the representation of virtues as types or models of good actions, and the teaching of the Ten Commandments, in which good actions are not simply indicated but also prescribed. This is irrespective of the fact that the Ten Commandments generally prohibit immoral actions rather than command virtuous ones. The commandment 'Honour thy father and mother' demands the virtue of respect.

Instead of agitating artificial conflicts between the two ways of considering morals, that is, between the ethics of virtues and the ethics of duties, it is far more useful and sensible to begin to realize that these two sets of morals represent two different but not opposed points of view. These enable one to judge what is right or wrong in the behaviour of individuals considered both for themselves, and in their mutual relations. And their clear contrast, as if one set of ethics could exclude the other, derives solely from an incorrect perspective of the observer. The objective of both sets of morals is a good action, whose motive is the search for, and whose goal is the attainment of Good. Except for this difference: that while the former describes, indicates and proposes it as an example, the latter prescribes the action as behaviour that must be followed, or regarded as a duty. The various short treatises on virtues and those *De officiis* complement each other, in the theoretical considera-tion of morals as well as in the moral teaching. Similarly, the catalogues of cardinal virtues and charitable deeds also complement rather than contrast each other in the teaching of morals in school, where from infancy these are com-mended to us in the form of precepts. The lives of eminent figures, of heroes and saints, which promote good deeds by pointing to examples of virtuous individuals, emerge from the tradition of the ethics of virtue. Conversely, legal ethics produce the kind of teaching that induces individuals to act correctly by proposing models for good actions. Their efficacy is cumulatively, rather than alternatively, different. Accordingly, instead of contrasting virtues with rules, it would be far wiser to analyse their relationship or the differ-ent rather than opposite practical needs which they emerge from and in turn obey.

Similarly and concurrently with the revival of the subject of virtues, which seemed to have disappeared from philo-sophical debate, the subject of the passions was also resur-rected. This, however, occurred with a different intellectual vigour, breadth of historical knowledge, and originality of outcomes, but with a similar intent for the antirationalist argument, through Remo Bodei's monumental work, *Geo-metria delle passioni*.[2] With regard to the reappraisal of virtues, Bodei's work is somewhat the obverse of the coin. While the ethics of virtue taught moderation, and therefore disciplining the passions (*pleonaxía*, the insatiable longing for possessions, represented moral sin in classical ethics, p. 17), Bodei asks whether we should revise the antithesis 'passion–reason', and reinstate the passions in their rightful place in the reconstruction and understanding of history, particularly in contemporary society where 'desires' occupy an increasingly greater space. Those desires consist of 'passions of expectancy for resources and satisfaction envisaged in the future' (p. 20). Among other things, Bodei also draws our attention to Hume's distinction between subdued or cold passions, and emotional or hot passions. As will become evident, in order to define 'meekness' I introduce the distinction between strong and weak virtues, which compared with the above is symmetrical.

I wish to also add that another reason for my consideration of this topic was the recent though uncommon use of the category of 'meekness' applied to 'law', which even as a mature reader of legal texts, I had not yet encountered. I am referring to Gustavo Zagrebelsky's *Il diritto mite*, which prior to reviewing required one to ask: 'Why meek?'.[3]

The friends who extended the invitation to me knew that I had not hesitated in choosing 'my' virtue. My only uncertainty concerned the choice of the term to use: 'meekness' or 'mildness'. Ultimately I chose 'meekness' for two reasons. In the Beatitudes (Matthew V:5), where it states 'Blessed are the meek for they shall inherit the earth', the Latin Vulgate text has *mites* [meek] instead of *mansueti* [mild]. The reason why this translation was adopted is unknown to me. It is one of the many questions that I leave in abeyance, and of which my unpretentious discussion is also replete. The second reason is that 'mild', at least originally, is understood to refer to animals rather than persons, even if figuratively it is also said of persons. (The same applies to 'meek': meek as a lamb. However, an animal is meek because it is domesticated, whereas a lamb is by nature the symbol of meekness.) The decisive argument comes from the respective verbs: to domesticate, to tame, or to render docile, which nearly exclusively refer to animals. In fact, one can correctly say 'to tame a tiger', and only jokingly 'to tame a mother-in-law'. In Dante's work one reads that Orpheus tamed the wild beasts. Instead 'mitigate', which derives from 'meek', refers almost exclusively to human acts, attitudes, actions, and passions. In other words, it means to mitigate the rigour of a law, the severity of a sentence, physical or moral pain, anger, rage, disdain, resentment, or the zeal of passion. For example, the following phrase may appear in a dictionary: 'Over time, the hatred between the two nations was mitigated.' However, it would be silly to say 'the hatred . . . was tamed'.

As far as the two abstract nouns that designate the respective virtues of 'mildness' and 'meekness' are concerned, I would say (but, since this is not a rigorous discussion, it is more an impression than a conviction) that meekness goes deeper, whereas mildness seems more superficial. More precisely, meekness is active, mildness passive. Mildness is more of a personal virtue, meekness a social virtue. Social in the sense that Aristotle differentiated personal virtues, such as courage and moderation, from the highest social virtue, which is justice. This is a positive inclination towards others, whereas courage and moderation are only positive attitudes towards oneself. Mildness is an individual's inward inclination, which can be appreciated as a virtue irrespective of one's relation with others. A mild person is calm and peaceful, someone who is not offended by minor issues, and who lives and allows others to live their life. He does not overreact to wanton malice, which is not because of weakness but out of a conscious acceptance of society's ills. Meekness instead is an inward inclination that radiates only in the presence of the other. A meek person is someone needed by others to help them defeat the evil within themselves.

The Turinese philosopher Carlo Mazzantini, belonged to the generation preceding mine and is no longer prominent. Despite the gap in our different understanding about the task of philosophers he is very dear to me for his deep philosophical vocation. In his writings, I discovered a tribute to and a definition of meekness that I found striking. Meekness, he states, is the only supreme 'power' (note how the word 'power' is used to designate a virtue that reminds one of the opposite, that is, powerlessness, but mind you, not resigned powerlessness). Observing that power consists 'of letting the other be himself', he adds: 'A violent person has no power, because by using violence he disempowers those who wish to give of themselves. Whereas power rests in those who possess the will that does not yield to violence, but is expressed through meekness.' 'To let the other be himself' therefore is a social virtue in the intrinsic and original meaning of the term.

Another linguistic observation is that the Italian language inherited the words 'meek' and 'meekness' from Latin. The French language has *mansuétude*. Also in French *doux* (and *douceur*) are used in nearly all the instances where the Italian uses 'meek', as for example: a *caractère doux*, an *hiver doux*. When Montesquieu compares the Japanese people, considered to have a cruel nature, with the Indian people, whose nature is regarded as *doux*, we translate it as 'meek', and in Italian this seems more precise. If we rendered it as 'sweet', we could do so without any disrespect to the language, but that would be considered a case of Gallicism. It would be something not altogether familiar, as with the chapter titled 'Mildness of punishment' in Beccaria's famous *Of Crimes and Punishment*, where the preferred translation of the word in Italian is 'meekness'. Beyond these linguistic observations, which although brief are sufficient to provide some indication of the problem before us, the fundamental theme that will be developed is the location of the virtue of meekness within the phenomenology of virtues.

Beside the classic distinction between individual and social virtues, there are others I have not considered. One of them, also classic, is the distinction between ethical and dianoetic virtues (meekness is certainly an ethical virtue), or yet another is that between theological and cardinal virtues introduced by Christian ethics (meekness is certainly a cardinal virtue). Instead it seems appropriate to introduce a distinction, which may or may not already have been made, between strong and weak virtues. Of course, in this context 'strong' and 'weak' do not correspond with the positive and negative connotation, respectively. It is an analytical rather than an axiological distinction. Rather than using a definition, I will try to convey to you what I mean by 'strong virtues' and 'weak virtues' by providing some examples. On the one hand there are virtues such as courage, steadfastness, prowess, daring, fearlessness, foresight, generosity, liberality, and clemency, which are typical of the powerful (we could also call them 'regal' or 'high-class' virtues, and perhaps, no ill-will intended, even 'aristocratic'). In other words, they are virtues practised by those who have the task of governing, directing, commanding, leading, and who are responsible for creating and maintaining nation-states. In effect, those virtues are likely to become evident above all in political life, and (depending on the viewpoint held) in that sublimation or perversion of politics that is war.

On the other hand, there are the virtues of humility, modesty, moderation, shyness, demureness, chastity, continence, sobriety, temperance, decency, innocence, naiveté, purity, simplicity, and among them also mildness, gentleness, and meekness, which are inherent to private, insignificant, or inconspicuous individuals. These are the persons located at the lower end of the social order, who have no control over anyone and, sometimes, not even over themselves. They are also those persons who go unnoticed, leaving no trace in the archives where only the records of outstanding protagonists and memorable deeds are preserved. The reason why I use the term 'weak' for these virtues is not because I consider them inferior, less useful or noble and therefore to be appreciated less, but because they characterize that section of society where the poor, and those who are humiliated and hurt, are situated. Moreover, these are the subjects who will never become rulers, who die without leaving any other trace of their presence on this earth than a cross in a cemetery bearing their name and a date. Then there are those who, because they make no history, are ignored by historians. But they represent a different history (written with a lower-case 'h'), the submerged history, or even worse, non-history. (Although there has been a debate for some time now, about a micro-history as opposed to macro-history, and it could well be that in such micro-history there is a place for them also.) I am reminded of Hegel's remarkable pages about those individuals in universal history, the state-builders whom he terms 'heroes'. These are individuals who are allowed to do what the common person is not permitted, even to use violence. Among them, there is no place for the meek. Woe betide the meek, for they will not inherit the earth. I am thinking of some of the most common epitaphs that fame has conferred on the powerful, such as magnanimous, great, victorious, bold, reckless, as well as terrible and bloodthirsty. But have you ever seen the name of a meek person in this gallery of the powerful? Someone suggested Ludwig the Affable. This title, however, is one that confers little glory.

To complete these observations, it would be useful to peruse some literary texts belonging to the *Specula principis*, and thus compile an exhaustive list of those virtues that are considered qualities and prerogatives of a good ruler. I selected Erasmus's *The Education of a Christian Prince* (the anti-Machiavellian, or the reverse of the 'demonic face of power'). Here we have the supreme virtues of the ideal prince: clemency, kindness, equity, civility, benevolence, as well as prudence, integrity, sobriety, temperance, vigilance, generosity, and honesty. It should be noted that nearly all are virtues that I termed 'weak'. The Christian prince is the opposite of Machiavelli's prince, or Hegel's hero (remembering that Hegel was a great admirer of Machiavelli). Nevertheless, I could not locate meekness, other than with reference to punishment, which must be 'mild' (however, on the basis of the old but always new argument that the infected limb must be removed to prevent the healthy part becoming contaminated, the death penalty is not excluded). Since any virtue can be more successfully defined if one keeps in mind its opposite vice, the opposite of meekness, when referring to punishment as meek or mild, is severity or rigour. Thus 'meekness' in the accepted meaning of the word can also be rendered as 'leniency'. However, this is certainly not the meaning adopted in my present defence of the virtue.

Other opposites of meekness, as I understand it, are arrogance, haughtiness, and domination, which depending on the different interpretations can be either the virtues or vices of politicians. Meekness is not a political virtue; rather it is the most apolitical of virtues. In the predominant meaning of politics, that is, the Machiavellian or the updated Schmittian version, meekness is exactly the opposite side of politics. In fact, it is for this reason (perhaps a professional aberration) that it is of special interest to me. One cannot cultivate political philosophy without trying to understand what is beyond politics, or without venturing into the non-political sphere, and attempting to establish the boundaries between the political and non-political. Politics is not everything. The idea that everything is politics is simply outrageous. I can say that I discovered meekness during my extended journey of exploration beyond politics. However, in the political or even democratic struggle, meaning by the latter the struggle for power that does not resort to violence, the meek have no part. As is well known, the two animals that symbolize the politician are the fox and the lion (refer to chapter XVIII of *The Prince*). The 'meek' lamb is not a political animal. If anything, it is the predestined victim sacrificed by the powerful to appease the demons of history. A maxim of popular wisdom states: 'Those who behave like sheep shall be eaten by the wolf.' The wolf is also a political animal: Hobbes's *homo homini lupus* [man a wolf to men] in the state of nature is the starting point for politics, and the *princeps principi lupus* [prince a wolf to princes] represents its continuation in international relations.

First of all meekness is the opposite of arrogance, understood as the exaggerated conception of one's merits, which justifies the abuse of power. A meek person does not have a high opinion of himself, not because of a lack of self-esteem, but due to his propensity to believe more in the lowly rather than lofty nature of humankind, and because he shares that humanity. Even more so, meekness is the contrary of haughtiness, which is showy arrogance. A meek person does not show off in any way, including his meekness. In other words, ostentation or the flaunting of one's supposed virtues in a blatant or impertinent manner is in itself a vice. Thus a pretended virtue is transformed into its opposite. Those who pretend to be charitable lack charity. Those who act as if they are intelligent are usually stupid. Quite rightly, therefore, meekness is the opposite of aggressiveness. I say, 'quite rightly', because compared with haughtiness, aggressiveness is even worse. It is abuse of power, not only feigned but also effectively exercised. Aggressive individuals exhibit their domineering nature, or the power to subdue others in manifold ways, for instance, as if swatting a fly or squashing a worm. Arrogant individuals exercise their power through all kinds of abuse and outrage, or acts of arbitrariness and, when necessary, ruthless domination. The meek, instead, 'let others be themselves' irrespective of whether these individuals may be arrogant, haughty, or domineering. They do not engage with others intending to compete, harass, and ultimately prevail. They refrain from exercising the spirit of contest, competition, or rivalry, and therefore also of winning. In life's struggle meek persons are perpetual losers. Their conception of the world and of history, or more precisely, of the only world and history they would want to inhabit, is one where there are neither winners nor losers. This is because in this kind of world there are no contests for primacy, no struggles for power and no competitions for wealth. In short, here the very conditions that enable the division of individuals into winners and losers do not exist.

Nevertheless, having reached this point of the discussion, I would not like anyone to confuse meekness with submissiveness. When defining a concept, one can use two methods. Either the method of opposition (for example, peace is the opposite of war), or the method of analogy (peace is analogous to a truce but also different from a truce). I will employ the same expedient to identify meekness as a virtue. Having defined meekness through the process of opposition, I will now try to refine it through the method of analogy with those virtues which are considered akin (but different) to it.

A submissive person is someone who abandons the struggle, due to weakness, fear, or resignation. A meek person does not yield. The meek repudiate the destructive life contest out of a sense of annoyance or for the futility of its intended aims. Their rejection might also be caused by a deep sense of detachment from those things that generate greed in most people, or due to a lack of that sentiment, which according to Hobbes was one of the reasons for 'the war of all against all'. That sentiment can be identified with vanity or pride that urges individuals to want to stand out. Finally, that rejection by the meek may be due to the total absence of stubbornness or obstinacy, which perpetuate quarrels over even trifling matters, by a succession of reciprocal grudges and reprisals expressed through the usual justification 'you did that to me, so I do this to you'. It may also be due to their lack of a feuding spirit or revenge, which inevitably leads either to one party prevailing over the other or to their mutual killing. The meek, then, are neither submissive nor yielding, because yielding reflects the attitude of those who have accepted the logic of the contest and rules of the game, where ultimately there are winners and losers (according to the theory of games, this is the zero-sum game). The meek do not hold grudges; they are not vindictive, nor are they resentful. They do not persist in brooding over past offences, or rekindle hatreds or reopen old wounds. To be at peace with oneself, one must first be at peace with others. The meek are never first to start the fire, and when others do, they refuse to let themselves be burnt, even when they are unable to extinguish the fire. They traverse the fire unscathed, and endure internal storms without becoming angry, maintaining their moderation, composure, and openness.

The meek are calm but, I repeat, not submissive persons. Nor are they affable, because in affability there is a certain impudence or incivility in judging others. An affable person is rather simple, or generally not smart enough to suspect the possible malice of others. I have no doubt whatsoever that meekness is a virtue. However, I cannot assert the same for affability, because an affable person does not have a balanced relationship with others (for this reason, if it is a virtue, it is passive).

Furthermore, is meekness to be confused with humility (humility raised to a virtue by Christianity)? Spinoza defines humility as *tristitia orta ex eo quod homo suam impotentiam sive imbecillitatem contemplatur* (a sadness arising from the fact that man contemplates his impotence or weakness). This sadness (*tristitia*) is in turn defined as *transitio a maiore ad minorem perfectionem* (the passage from a higher to a lower perfection). The difference between meekness and humility consists, in my view, of that *tristitia* (sadness). Meekness is not a form of 'sadness', because it is rather its opposite, *laetitia*, which is understood as the passage from a lower to a higher perfection. The meek are cheerful because they are inwardly convinced that the world to which they aspire is better than the one they are forced to inhabit. They anticipate that world by effectively exercising the virtue of meekness through their daily activity, fully aware that it does not exist here and now, and that perhaps it never will. Yet another opposite of humility is excessive self-satisfaction, or simply put, swollen pride. As already mentioned, the opposite of meekness is abuse of power, or in the literal sense of the word, oppression. A meek person can be depicted as the precursor of a better world, whereas the humble person is only a witness, quite noble yet without hope, of this future world.

Even less can meekness be mistaken for modesty. Modesty is characterized by an underestimation of oneself, which is not always honest but rather often even hypocritical. Meekness is neither underestimation nor overestimation of oneself, because it is not an attitude towards oneself, but always in respect of others, and its only justification rests in 'being an expression towards the other'. This does not exclude the fact that a meek person can also be humble and modest. But the three aspects do not coincide. We are humble and modest for ourselves. We are meek in respect of others.

As a way of expressing oneself towards others, meekness borders the region of tolerance and of respect for the ideas and lifestyle of others. Yet a meek person is not just tolerant and respectful. Because tolerance is reciprocal, in order for tolerance to be exercised there must be at least two persons. When one person tolerates the other, we witness the condition of tolerance. If I tolerate you but you do not tolerate me, there is no condition of tolerance, but on the contrary there is domination. The same applies to respect. Kant maintains that

'Every person has the right to expect the respect of his own kind, and he himself is *reciprocally* obliged to respect others.' A meek person does not ask for or expect any reciprocity. Meekness is an attitude towards others that does not need to be reciprocated for it to be fully actualized. This is also the case with altruism, kindness, generosity, and mercy, all of which are social as well as unilateral virtues. This should not appear contradictory in that they are unilateral virtues, because the expression of one person towards the other does not correspond with the analogous expression, be that the same or contrary, of the second person towards the first, as in 'I will tolerate you if you tolerate me.' Instead a meek person would say: 'I safeguard and value my meekness, generosity or kindness towards you, irrespective of the fact that you may also be meek, generous, or kind towards me.' Tolerance emerges from an agreement and will endure as long as that agreement is kept. Meekness, instead, is a gift and has no predetermined or prescribed limits.

To complete the picture, there is a need to consider that alongside the kindred virtues, there are also the complementary virtues, which are those that can be used together and thus strengthen each other. In relation to meekness, two come to mind: simplicity and charity (or compassion). Except for this cautionary remark in that simplicity is the necessary, or almost, precondition for meekness, and meekness is a possible precondition for compassion. In other words, to be meek one must be simple, and only the meek can be well disposed towards compassion. By 'simplicity' I mean the shunning of useless abstruseness on the intellectual level and ambiguous positions in practice. If you wish, you can think of simplicity as being combined with lucidity, or clarity, or the rejection of simulation. Understood in this sense, it seems to me that simplicity is a precondition or rather a predisposition for meekness. Seldom can complicated individuals be well disposed towards meekness. They see intrigues, plots, and traps everywhere, and are as diffident of others as they are insecure of themselves.

With regard to the relationship between meekness and compassion, I do not consider that as a necessary but only as a possible relationship, meaning that meekness cannot be an inclination towards mercy. But, as Aldo Capitini[4] would have maintained, mercy is an 'addition'. It is so obviously an addition that among all living beings only humans comprehend the virtue of mercy. Mercy is a feature of a human being's pre-eminence, dignity, and uniqueness. How many of the virtues have been symbolized by an animal! Among other things, some of those evoked by this discussion are: simple as a dove, meek as a lamb, the noble steed, the gentle gazelle, the courageous and generous lion, and the faithful dog. Have you ever tried to imagine the virtue of mercy as an animal? You can try, but you may find it difficult. Vico maintained that the civilized world emerged from men's sense of shame, who, when terrified by Jupiter's thunderbolt, abandoned the fair Venus and took their women into the caves. Even if we accept that the civilized world emerged from a sense of shame, only mercy marks the human from the animal world, or from the non-human domain of nature. Sometimes, even in the human world, we can find that 'compassion failed' (*pietà l'è morta*, as a partisan song familiar to those of my generation stated). In the animal world compassion cannot fail because there it is unknown.

I feel obliged to conclude these swift observations by explaining the reasons why, when confronted with the rather extensive catalogue of virtues, I specifically chose meekness.

You have probably been thinking that I chose meekness because I consider it particularly congenial to me. I must honestly confess that this was not the case. I would like to have the nature of a meek person, but this is not so. I go into a fury far too often to consider myself a meek person (I relate my feeling to 'fury' rather than to 'heroic fury'). It is true that I love meek persons, because it is they that make this 'flower bed' more habitable. This realization prompted me to think that the ideal city may not be that imagined and described in every detail by utopians, where the prevailing justice is so rigid and stern as to be intolerable. Instead, it might be a city where the kindness in the customs becomes universal practice (like the China idealized by eighteenth-century writers). Moreover, judging from my depiction, meekness has probably appeared to you as a feminine virtue. I fully accept this. I am aware that, by saying that meekness has always seemed desirable to me precisely because of its femininity, I am disappointing all those women who stood up against centuries-old male domination. I believe the practice of kindness is bound to prevail when the city of women is realized (not Fellini's, of course). For this reason I feel that I have never encountered anything more annoying than the warning expressed by the most adamant feminists, which stated: 'Tremble and shiver, the witches have come hither.' I can understand the polemic meaning of such an expression, but it is nevertheless unpleasant.

My choice of meekness, therefore, is not a biographic selection. Of itself it is a metaphysical choice, because it is grounded in a conception of the world that I could not otherwise justify. However, from the viewpoint of the circumstances that prompted it, it is an historical choice. In other words, it can be considered a reaction to the violent society in which we are forced to live. It is not that I am so devoid of worldly experience as to believe that human history has always been an idyll. Rather, it was once defined by Hegel as 'a huge slaughterhouse'. Today, however, there are 'megatons', which represent the ultimate development for 'the fate of the earth' (to use Jonathan Schell's book title). Now the experts inform us that with all the weapons accumulated in the arsenals of the superpowers, it is possible to destroy the earth many times over. The fact that this is possible does not mean it must necessarily occur. Even if a nuclear war were unleashed, the experts still claim that the earth would not be destroyed completely. Just think for a moment, though, what a difficult task it would be to start all over again! What terrifies me is those dreaded megatons combined with the persisting will for power. However, it seems that in the twentieth century, the century with two world wars, and the Cold War between the two superpowers that lasted forty years, the will for power increased and was sublimated. That will for power is not only exhibited by the great powers. There is also that power of smaller entities. These include the lone assassin, the small terrorist group, or someone who throws a bomb into a crowd, or in a bank, a crowded train, or a waiting room where it can cause the death of the largest possible number of innocent people. It is the will for power of whoever identifies with this self-justification: 'I, a humble, insignificant, and obscure person, can kill someone important, or a protagonist of our time, and as a result I am more powerful than he. With a single blow, I may kill many insignificant and obscure individuals like myself, but who are absolutely innocent. In other words, to kill a guilty party is an act of justice, but to kill innocent victims is the extreme manifestation of the will for power'.

I trust you have understood me: I identify the meek person with the nonviolent, and meekness with the refusal to exercise violence against anyone. Meekness, therefore, is a non-political virtue. Even more so, in a world bloodstained by the hatred of the great (and small) powers, meekness is the antithesis of politics.

Notes

1. A. MacIntyre, *After Virtue: A Study in Moral Theory* (London, Duckworth 1981). Refer also to S. Natoli, *Dizionario dei vizi e delle virtù* [*Dictionary of Vices and Virtues*], (Milan, Feltrinelli 1996).
2. R. Bodei, *Geometria delle passioni* [*A Geometry of Passions*] (Milan, Feltrinelli 1991).
3. G. Zagrebelsky, *Il diritto mite* [*The Meek Law*] (Turin, Einaudi 1992).
4. [Translator's note: Aldo Capitini (1899–1968) was a defiant philosopher, idealist, and liberal-socialist thinker. His aversion to fascism as a prototype of a closed society was principally morally inspired, but after the *Concordat* (reconciliation between the church and the fascist state) in 1929, it was also religious. He contended that there was a need to go beyond the contrast between capitalism and communism, and use non-violence and non-cooperation as the basis for antifascist struggle. He was deeply influenced by Gandhi's thought and actions. In the realist tradition of Italian political thought, the ideal of nonviolence was the absolute novelty of Capitini's work. (See

N. Bobbio, preface, 'Cinquant'anni dopo' ['Fifty years on'], in A. Capitini, *Elementi di un'esperienza religiosa* [*Principles of a Religious Experience*], (Bologna, Cappelli 1990), pp. v–xx. For my translation of 'Preface' refer to *Convivio* (1996), 2(2), October, pp. 128–40.]

Part I

Ethics and Politics

Posing the question

The increasingly more frequent debates on the moral question occurring in Italy in recent years repropose the old problem of the relation between morals and politics. This is an old yet perennially new subject, because there is no moral question that may be advanced in any field for which a definitive solution has ever been found. While its importance derives from a number of factors, such as the antiquity of the debate, the authority of the authors, the variety of the arguments, and the significance of the subject, the question of the relation between morals and politics is no different from that of the relation between morals and all other human activities. In this respect we generally speak of ethics in economic relations, or as in recent years, of ethics of the market, of sexual ethics, medical ethics, sports ethics, and so on. However, the concern is always with the same problem in all these different spheres of human activity: the distinction between what is morally right and what is morally wrong.

The question of the relations between ethics and politics is far more serious, as the lessons of history have shown, at least since the conflict between Antigone and Creon. Moreover, common sense seems to have accepted willingly that a politician can behave in a way that differs from common morals. Thus, an act that is morally wrong can be regarded and appreciated as right in politics. In short, it is accepted that politics obey a code of rules, or a normative system, different from, and partly incompatible with, the code or normative system for moral behaviour. Machiavelli (almost approvingly) attributes the maxim that states are not governed by divine entreaty (with the *pater noster* in hand) to Cosimo de' Medici. This reveals that he also considers as a given that a politician cannot pursue his activity by following the prevailing moral principles, which in a Christian society also happen to coincide with evangelical morals. A contemporary example of this is depicted by Jean-Paul Sartre in his well-known drama *Les mains sâles*, where the author, or rather one of the protagonists, maintains that those who engage in political activity cannot avoid staining their hands (with dirt or even blood).

Despite the fact, therefore, that the moral question is present in all areas of human behaviour, when the moral question is raised in the sphere of politics it assumes a very special characteristic. In all the other areas, the moral question consists of debating what is a morally right behaviour and, conversely, what is morally wrong. And in the case of non-rigorist morals, which are no different, in economic, sexual, or sporting relations, and in those between doctor and patient, or teacher and student, and so on. The debate focuses on the principles or rules that entrepreneurs or traders, lovers or married couples, poker or soccer players, doctors, surgeons, and teachers must follow in conducting their activities. What is not usually questioned is the moral question, or whether such a question exists. In other words, whether it is plausible to consider the problem of morality of the respective behaviours. Let us take, for example, the field where for years a particularly lively debate has raged among moralists, of medical ethics and of bio-ethics more generally. While the argument is fairly animated with regard to the wrongfulness or otherwise of certain actions, no one would ever think of rejecting the problem itself. The fact is that in medical practice problems emerge, which are usually regarded as moral by all those involved. Accordingly, these practitioners understand each other well, even though they may not agree on the principles to be observed and the rules to be applied. It is no different to what is happening in the current dispute on the morality of the market. Where the market is regarded as a rationally perfect mechanism having a spontaneous rather than a reflected rationality, it cannot be subjected to moral evaluation.[1] There the question is posed in the same way as is traditionally considered for the moral question in politics, except for this difference. Even in the most morally objective evaluations of the market, it would be impossible to reach the point where one could consciously or by reasoning support the immorality of the market. At best, one could accept its pre-morality or amorality. It is not so much that the market is incompatible with morals, but rather the fact that it is extraneous to any moral judgement. A staunch supporter of the market does not need to argue that the market is not governed by divine entreaty. If anything, he asserts that it cannot be governed at all.

Naturally, the issue of the relations between morals and politics can only make sense if there is agreement in maintaining that morals exist, and that by and large certain characterizing principles are accepted. In order to agree on the existence of morals and some very general principles, such as the negative *neminem laedere* [hurt no one] and the positive *suum cuique tribuere* [give to each their own], it is not necessary to agree on their foundation. This is above all the foremost philosophical subject that has always divided philosophical schools, and will continue so to do. The relation between the different types of ethics and ethical theory is quite complex. Here we can simply say that disagreement on the foundations does not prejudice the agreement on fundamental rules.

If there is a need, this is to explain that when one discusses morals in relation to politics, one refers to the social rather than to the personal aspect of morals. Social morals are those concerned with the actions of an individual that may interfere with the sphere of activity of other individuals. Personal morals, on the other hand, concern those actions relative to perfecting one's personality, irrespective of the consequences that the pursuit of this ideal may have on others. Traditional ethics have always differentiated between duties towards others and duties towards oneself. What is questioned in the debate on the issue of morals in politics is exclusively the duties towards others.

Can political activity be subjected to moral judgement?

Differently from other areas of human behaviour, in the sphere of politics the question that is traditionally posed does not concern which actions are morally right or wrong, but *if* there is any sense in asking the question of the moral rightness or wrongness of political actions. The following example will enable us to comprehend the difference better than a long dissertation. There is no moral system that does not contain principles aimed at preventing the use of violence and fraud. The two principal categories of offences provided for in our penal codes are crimes of violence and fraud. In a famous chapter of *The Prince*, Machiavelli maintains that a good politician must be adept at the skills of the lion and the fox. But these are the symbols of strength and craftiness.

In modern times the most Machiavellian of all modern writers, Vilfredo Pareto, who is also included among the Machiavellians in a well-known old text, recently brought back into circulation,[2] has no qualms in maintaining that politicians fall into two categories. The first comprises politicians with a predominant instinct for the persistence of aggregates, and these are Machiavelli's lions. The other category consists of those with a predominant instinct for combinations, and these are Machiavelli's foxes. Croce, who was an admirer of both Machiavelli and Marx for their realist conception of politics, in one of his famous pages develops the topic of 'political honesty'. He begins the discussion with the following words, which require no comment: 'A further demonstration of common ignorance regarding political matters is the insistent demand for honesty in political life.' After noting that this is the ideal that springs from the heart of idiots, he explains that 'political honesty is nothing more than political ability'.[3] This, we add, is what Machiavelli termed 'virtue', which as everyone knows has nothing at all to do with the type of virtue discussed in moral treatises beginning with Aristotle's *Nicomachean Ethics*.

It would seem from these examples, which could be multiplied, that the only conclusion to be drawn is the impossibility of posing the question of the relations between morals and politics in the same terms as it is posed in other spheres of human behaviour. And this is not due to the lack of supporting theories for the opposite thesis, namely, that even politics are subject, or rather should be subjected, to moral law. Such theories, however, could never become established through very convincing arguments, and have been regarded just as lofty as they were useless.

The subject of justification

Despite the attention given to the body of arguments, these would probably only have limited impact on the morality of politics. However, the majority of authors concerned with this issue became more aware of the lesson of history and shared experience from which one draws to understand the gap between common morals and political behaviour. Accordingly, they directed their attention to trying to understand, and ultimately justify, this divergence. I maintain that the whole, or at least the greater part, of the history of modern political thought can be summarized by the search for a solution of the moral issue in politics. This is interpreted as a series of attempts to provide a justification of the fact, by itself surprising, of the obvious difference between common morals and political morals. When political writers confront the issue in this way, they do not intend to provide prescriptions for politicians. Rather, they forgo the field of precepts, and instead attempt to understand the phenomenon from a different perspective. Today, given the prevailing distinction between ethics and meta-ethics, the greater number of investigations on the morality of politics that abound in modern political philosophy are mostly concerned with meta-ethics, although they cannot avoid some unintentional secondary reflections on ethics.

I speak about 'justification' after careful consideration. The behaviour that needs to be justified is one that does not conform to the rules. It is not necessary to justify the observance of norms, that is, moral behaviour. However, the need for justification emerges when an action violates, or appears to violate, commonly accepted social rules, be they moral, legal, or customary. Obedience does not need to be justified, but disobedience does, where it is considered to have some moral value. Likewise, one's attendance at a mandatory meeting needs no justification, but one's absence does. Generally, there is no need to justify a regular or normal action, whereas it is necessary to provide a justification for an action that exceeds or falls short of expectation, if one wants to safeguard it. No one asks for justification of a mother's action in jumping into the river to save her child from drowning. But a justification is expected should she not do so. The question of theodicy, one of the major theological and metaphysical questions, emerges from observing the presence of evil in the world and throughout history. Candide does not strive to justify the existence of the best of possible worlds. If anything, his task is to explain or demonstrate why the world is this and not that way.

When confronted with the vastness of the topic, the task I set myself is quite modest. So I thought it might be useful to provide, as an introduction, a 'map' of the different and contrasting solutions that have been given historically to this problem of the relation between ethics and politics.

It concerns a map that is certainly incomplete and imperfect because it is open to the possibility of a dual error. The first is regarding the classification of the types of solution, and the other concerns the framing of the different solutions in each respective type. The first error is of a conceptual nature, and the other of historical interpretation. It is therefore a map that needs revising by further observations. But in the meantime I believe it can provide at least an initial orientation for those who, prior to venturing into an unknown territory, want to become acquainted with all the paths that traverse it.

All the examples are drawn from modern political philosophy, from Machiavelli on. While it is true that all the important political philosophy begins in Greece, the debate about the problem of the relations between ethics and politics becomes particularly intense with the formation of the modern state. And for the first time it is given the name of 'reason of state', which will never desert it.

What is the reason for this? I advance the following, albeit quite cautiously. The dualism between ethics and politics is one of the aspects of the great clash between church and state. Such dualism could only emerge from the contrast between an institution whose mission is one of teaching, preaching, and commending universal laws of behaviour, which were revealed by God, and an earthly institution whose task is to guarantee temporal order in human relations. The clash between ethics and politics in the modern age is, in effect, resolved from the outset through the clash between Christian morals and the praxis of those who undertake political activity. In a pre-Christian state, where morals have not been institutionalized, the clash is less obvious. This does not mean that Greek thought ignored it. Suffice to think of the conflict between the unwritten laws that inspired Antigone and the laws of the tyrant. But in the Greek world there is not just one, but different kinds of morals. Each philosophical school has its own set of morals. Wherever there are different kinds of morals with which political activity can be compared, the problem of the relation between morals and politics no longer has a precise meaning. What prompted the interest of Greek thought was not so much the problem of the relation between ethics and politics, but the problem of the relation between good and bad government, from which the distinction between king and tyrant emerges. But this is a distinction within the political system that does not concern the relation between a normative system, such as politics, and another normative system consisting of morals. Instead, that is what happens in the Christian and post-Christian world.

The second reason for my choice is that due to the formation of large territorial states, politics became increasingly the arena where the will for power is explicated. This is a bigger theatre and thus much more visible than that of the minor

city feuds, or the conflicts in feudal society. This is especially
the case when the will for power is placed at the service of a
religious faith. The debate on the reason of state flares up
during the period of the wars of religion. The clash between
morals and politics reveals all its intensity when morally
reprehensible actions (consider the notable example of the
night of St Bartholomew, which was praised by, among
others, the Machiavellian Gabriel Naudé) are committed in
the name of God, as the original, unique, and exclusive
source for the moral order of the world.

A third reason can also be added. It is not until the sixteenth century that the clash is also recognized as a practical
problem and attempts are made to provide some explanation.
Once again the canonical text is Machiavelli's *The Prince*, in
particular chapter XVIII. It begins with the prophetic words:

> Everyone recognizes how praiseworthy it is for a ruler to keep
> his word, and to live a life of integrity, without relying on
> craftiness. Nevertheless, we see that in practice, in these days,
> those rulers who have not thought it important to keep their
> word have achieved great things, and have known how to
> employ cunning to confuse and disorientate other men. In
> the end, they have been able to overcome those who have
> placed store in integrity.

The key to it all is the expression 'great things'. If one starts to
discuss the problem of human action from the point of view
of 'great things', that is, outcomes, rather than from the point
of view of principles, then the moral question changes completely. It is radically overturned. The extended debate on the
reason of state is a commentary, which persisted for centuries, of this peremptory and unmistakably truthful statement:
that in political activity what counts are not principles but
great things.

Returning to our typology, following this premise, I will
add yet another. Among the theories on ethics and politics
that I will discuss, some will have a predominantly prescriptive value, in that they do not claim to explain the clash, but
aim to provide a practical solution for it. Others have a
predominantly analytical value in that they do not simply

propose how relations between ethics and politics should be resolved, but aim to indicate what is the reason for the existence of the clash. I maintain that the lack of consideration of the different function of the theories has led to a great deal of confusion. For example, there is no sense in refuting a prescriptive theory by making realist observations. Similarly, it makes no sense to oppose an analytical theory by proposing a better or the best solution of the clash.

I divide the theories that have considered the question of the relation between morals and politics into four major groups, even if in effect they are not always clearly separable, and in fact often converge into each other. I differentiate monist from dualist theories; in turn, the monist theories into rigid and flexible monism; and the dualist theories into apparent and real dualism. Falling within rigid monism are those authors for whom there is no clash between morals and politics, because there is only one normative system, either moral or political. Flexible monism comprises authors for whom there is only one normative system, the moral, which in extraordinary circumstances or for specific subjects nevertheless allows derogations or exceptions justifiable by arguments that belong to the sphere of the reasonable. Apparent dualism includes those authors who conceive morals and politics as two distinct normative systems not totally independent of each other, but superimposed on each other hierarchically. Finally, within real dualism there are authors for whom morals and politics are two different normative systems that obey different evaluation criteria. I have outlined the different theories according to the progressively greater gap between the two normative systems.

Rigid monism

Rigid monism is manifested in two versions, depending on whether the *reductio ad unum* is achieved by resolving politics in morals, or conversely, morals in politics.

An example of the first version is the idea, or rather the ideal, typical of the sixteenth century, of the Christian prince so well depicted in Erasmus's *The Education of a Christian Prince*, which dates back to 1515. The text is almost a contemporary of Machiavelli's *The Prince*, which is its most radical antithesis. Erasmus's Christian prince is the reverse of the demonic face of power. For example, when Erasmus addresses the prince, he states: 'If you want to show that you are an excellent prince, see that no one outdoes you in the necessary qualities of wisdom, magnanimity, restraint, and integrity.' These exclusively moral virtues have nothing to do with virtue understood in the Machiavellian sense. Moreover, Erasmus continues, 'If you want to compete with other princes, do not consider yourself superior to them if you take away part of their realm or rout their troops, but only if you have been less corrupt than they, less greedy, less arrogant, less irascible, and less impulsive.' Thereafter the prince asks: 'What then is my cross?', to which Erasmus replies: 'So long as you follow what is right, not to harm anyone, do violence to no one, extort from no one, sell no public office, and are corrupted by no bribes.' The prince's satisfaction rests in being just, not in 'great things'.

I draw the second example from Kant. In the appendix of that golden book *Perpetual Peace*, Kant distinguishes the political moralist, whom he censures, from the moral politician, whom he praises. A moral politician is someone who does not subject morals to the demands of politics. Instead, he interprets the principles of political caution in a way that allows them to coexist with morals. 'Although the maxim "Honesty is the best policy" implies a theory that unfortunately is quite often disproved by practice, the equally abstract maxim "Honesty is better than politics" is nevertheless infinitely superior to any objection, and constitutes the indispensable condition of politics.' It may be of interest for a moral scholar to know that both Erasmus and Kant, though starting from different moral theories, as far as the foundation of morals is concerned, resort to the same argument to support their thesis. In contemporary ethical theory this would be termed 'consequentialism', meaning that consequences are taken into account. Contrary to what is asserted by Machiavellians, for whom non-observance of prevailing moral rules is the condition for success, our two authors maintain that in the long term success favours the ruler who respects universal moral principles. It is like saying: 'Do good because it is your duty; but also because, irrespective of your intentions, your action will be rewarded.' It is evident that this is a fairly ordinary pedagogical argument with limited persuasive strength. We may as well admit it: it is a weak argument that is unsupported by either history or common experience.

As an example of the second version of monism, that is, of the reduction of morals to politics, I chose Hobbes, naturally here again with all due caution. Above all, since some recent critics have highlighted what has been termed 'the clarity full of confusion of the author of *Leviathan*'. They warn the reader, who may be enthralled or attracted by the logical strength of Hobbesian arguments, about interpretations that may be too unilateral. Nevertheless, it seems to me that in certain respects it is difficult to find an author with a more rigorous normative monism, and whose normative system, excluding all others, is the political system. This consists of the system of rules that derive from the will of the sovereign, who is legitimated by the social contract. Several arguments may be advanced. First for Hobbes, subjects do not have the right to judge what is just or unjust, since this belongs only to the sovereign. Thus to maintain that a subject has the right to judge what is just or unjust is considered a revolutionary notion. However, the fundamental argument is that Hobbes is one of the few authors, perhaps the only one, for whom there is no distinction between prince and tyrant. And there is no distinction because the possibility of differentiating between a good and bad government does not exist. Finally, since I referred to the clash between church and state as the determining contrast to understand the question of the reason of state in the fifteenth and sixteenth centuries, I raise the point that Hobbes reduces the church to the state. Accordingly, church laws are laws only in as much as they are accepted, wanted, and reinforced by the state. By denying the distinction between church and state, and reducing the church to the state, Hobbes eliminates the very reason for the contrast.

The theory of derogation

According to the theories of flexible monism there is only one normative system, and this is the moral system. This holds whether its foundation rests in a revelation or in nature and from which human reason is of its own accord capable of deriving universal laws of behaviour. Precisely because these laws are general, however, they cannot be applied in all cases. There is no moral law that does not foresee exceptions in particular circumstances. The rule 'Thou shalt not kill' defaults in the event of legitimate defence, that is, where violence is the only possible remedy against violence. In that particular circumstance it is based on the maxim *vim vi repellere licet* [it is permissible to repel force by force] that has been accepted expressly or tacitly by the majority of moral and legal normative systems. The rule, 'Do not lie' defaults, for example, in the case where a member of a revolutionary movement is arrested and asked to denounce his comrades. It is an established maxim in every legal system that *lex specialis derogat generali* [particular cases modify general law]. This is also valid in morals, and in those codified and contained in treatises of moral theology used by priests.

According to the theory being outlined here, what at first may seem a violation of the moral code committed by a political leader is in fact simply a derogation of the moral law effected in an exceptional circumstance. In other words, what justifies the violation is the exceptional nature of the situation in which the sovereign had to act. Since we are trying to identify the different reasons for justification of the non-moral behaviour of a politician, in this instance the reason is to be found not in presuming the existence of a different normative system, but in the only normative system accepted, within which the rule that provides for derogation in exceptional cases is considered valid. If anything, what characterizes a sovereign's behaviour is the extraordinary frequency of exceptional circumstances where he is compared to an ordinary person. That frequency is due to the fact that he acts in a web of relations, for example with other sovereigns, where the exception becomes a rule. This occurs despite the fact that it can be considered contradictory (but here it is not really contradictory, because it concerns a rule in the sense of regularity, and the regularity of a contrasting behaviour does not mean that it affects the validity of the given rule). Even if it seems that the derogation is always to the sovereign's advantage (and it is precisely this advantage that has been opposed by moralists), the reverse situation can also occur, although more rarely. In effect, derogation can have broad usage, in that it allows a sovereign to do something that is morally prohibited. But it can also be restrictive because it prohibits certain actions that are permitted to the ordinary person: *noblesse oblige*.

There is no need to discuss the historical importance of this justificatory reason much further. The theorists of the reason of state, who flourished during the seventeenth century and were responsible for the most intense and continuous reflection on the subject of the relations between politics and morals, were often jurists. To resolve the problem that Machiavelli placed on the agenda, it was natural for them to apply the well-known principle of derogation for exceptional circumstances in a state of necessity. As we shall soon see, that was achieved through a clearly dualist solution. Thus they were able to safeguard the principle of one moral code, and at the same time provide rulers with an argument to support their actions when violating that code. This, as Machiavelli outrageously discovered, served to conceal the 'demonic face of power'. Jean Bodin, Christian author and jurist, began his major work, *Six Books of the Commonwealth*, with an invective against Machiavelli (a ritual for a Christian writer). However, in the section where Bodin differentiates between king and tyrant, he maintains that 'One must not however label as evidence of tyranny the executions, banishments, confiscations, and other deeds of violence that mark a revolution or restoration in a commonwealth. Such changes are necessarily violent.'[4] Change and restoration of a regime are precisely those exceptional circumstances, or that state of necessity, which justifies actions that in normal circumstances would be considered immoral.

The theory of special ethics

To illustrate the second reason for justification of the gap between common morals and political behaviour I employ another legal category, the *ius singulare* [individual rule]. I am the first to acknowledge that these analogies between political and legal theories must be adopted with caution. But as a result of their extended theorization and constant application in legal case-studies, they provide starting points for reflection and practical suggestions in related fields, such as that of moral and political case-studies. Unlike the relation between rule and exception that concerns the peculiarity of a situation termed a 'state of necessity', the relation between *ius commune* [communal rule] and *ius singulare* concerns in the first place the specificity of actors. More precisely, it concerns the *status* of certain actors who, because of that status, enjoy or endure a different normative regime from that applicable to ordinary people. In this case also, one can speak of derogation of the common law. However, what distinguishes this type of derogation from that examined in the previous section is the reference not just to a type of situation but also to the type of actor. This is effective regardless of whether the typicality of the actor derives from the social condition, in that the legal system to which a noble is subject differs from that of someone from the middle class or of a peasant. It is also valid regardless of the activity undertaken, and can be illustrated by the well-known example of the development of commercial law, instituted over centuries as a 'derogation' of civil law.

When applied to the moral question, the category of *ius singulare* is quite useful as an introduction to professional ethics. This consists of that body of rules of behaviour which persons who undertake a particular activity must obey. These rules generally differ from those of the system that governs common morals, because they either exceed or do not fulfil expectations. That is to say, because they either impose more stringent obligations on members of a given association, or because they exempt those members from impractical obligations, such as in the case of a doctor telling the truth in the case of a terminally ill patient. There is nothing to stop professional ethics being called individual morals, in the same way as in legal theory one refers to individual rights. This is demonstrated by the fact that such practitioners love to attribute to them a specific term, particularly compelling for its solemnity, of 'deontology'.

Do those individuals who conduct a political activity constitute a body that can be likened to a profession or an association? Clearly, this does not mean taking up a position with respect to the current problem of 'political professionalism'. Rather, it seeks to ascertain whether political activity is an activity with such specific characteristics as to require a particular normative regime with the same rationale as any other type of professional ethics. That rationale is to enable the development of a particular activity to attain its essential goal. The goal of politics is the common good, in the same way as the doctor's objective is someone's health, and the priest's aspiration the salvation of souls. There is nothing strange in posing the question in these terms. The debate on the nature of political activity began in ancient Greece, and ever since it has been regarded as a skill, or a form of positive action (*poiéin*). It was also compared with other types of skill, which in order to achieve a good result required a specific competence. Plato's *Statesman*, whose aim is to explain what the substance of regal science is, or what is the intrinsic knowledge of someone who has to govern, is a learned comparison between the skill of government and that of the weaver. In any event the likeness, so frequent as to become a ritual, between the skill of government and that of the helmsman has left us the legacy of the term 'government' and its derivatives, which we use regularly without remembering its original meaning. Sometimes the comparison resurfaces in very different historical situations and contexts, such as the time when we learnt that Mao was called the 'Great Helmsman'.

Throughout the history of the debate on the reason of state there is also, alongside the justification of the 'immorality' of politics derived from the argument of the state of necessity, that derived from the nature of political activity. Such activity dictates certain morally reprehensible actions to whomever is involved in it, even when they are deemed necessary by both the nature and aim of that activity. If there are political ethics different to ethical ethics, according to this argument, that depends on the fact that a politician, like the doctor, the merchant, or the priest, could not perform his task without obeying the appropriate code. However, this code need not necessarily coincide with the code of common morals, or that of other professions. In this way, political ethics become the ethics of politicians, and inasmuch as they are inherent to politicians they are special ethics. As such, therefore, they can have justifiable reasons to approve of a behaviour that may seem immoral to an ordinary person, but to a philosopher it appears simply as the behaviour of an individual and member, necessarily conforming with the group's particular ethics. If we re-read Croce's passage, cited earlier, it becomes evident how the consideration of political skill as a profession among others has not lost any of its enduring vitality. By disapproving of the common and, in his view, incorrect demand by 'simpletons' that a politician should be honest, Croce remarks that:

> When it concerns caring for one's health or needing surgery no one asks for an honest man...yet everyone asks for, seeks, or engages doctors and surgeons, regardless of whether they are honest or dishonest, as long as they are competent in medicine or surgery....Instead, in political matters one does not ask for politicians [men who are capable and effective as politicians, I would add], but for honest men who at best may be endowed with different attitudes.

Croce continues: 'Hence it is obvious that if the shortcomings which a man with ability and political skill may possibly have concern other spheres of activity, then they may render him unfit for those spheres, but not for politics.'[5] I wish to draw your attention to the term 'unfit' that, by contrast, makes one think of a 'characteristic' of politics, which is not obviously that of morals.

The theory of the superiority of politics

I now move from conceptions of attenuated or corrected monism, 'there is only one morality but its validity does not hold in exceptional circumstances or in spheres of special activities', to a conception of avowed but objective dualism. I seek your forbearance for my persistent reference to legal categories, but even in this respect I am aided by a well-known jurisprudential principle, according to which when two rules are arranged hierarchically, if they are antinomies, the superior rule prevails.

With regard to the question of the relations between morals and politics, one of the possible solutions is to conceive morals and politics as two distinct normative systems but not altogether independent of each other, even if they are hierarchically arranged. Of course, this kind of solution can have two versions. In the two normative systems, either the moral is superior to the political, or the political is superior to the moral. A typical example of the first version is Croce's practical philosophy, and of the other, Hegel's philosophy. In Croce's system, economics and ethics are two distinctions, which are neither opposites nor located on the same level. Ethics are superior to economics in that they belong to the moment of the Spirit that *supersedes* the inferior moment. Politics belong to the sphere of economics rather than of ethics. This is not to say that 'to supersede' means that it is also axiologically superior. But in effect whenever Croce considers the Machiavellian problem of the relation between ethics and politics, he seems to accept that the difference between the two moments is an axiologically hierarchical difference, even if it is not always clear what its consequences might be. Is a political action contrary to morals to be condemned? What does it mean that it is legitimate within its particular sphere, if subsequently one admits that there is a normatively superior sphere? These are questions that I find difficult to answer. Croce revisits the issue on numerous occasions. Here I am referring to a passage in the volume, aptly titled *Ethics and Politics*, where he emphasizes a

particular point. The circle of politics is that of utility, business, negotiations, and struggles. In these continuous wars,
individuals, populations, and states remain vigilant against
other individuals, populations, and states intent on maintaining and promoting their existence, and respecting others only
in so far as it benefits them. Then, continuing his reasoning,
he cautions against the common error of separating the life
forms from each other. He urges the rejection of silly moral-
izations, and to consider false *a priori* any dissension one may
perceive between politics and morals, because political life is
either preparation for moral life, or itself the means of a form
of moral life. In short, according to Crocean dialectics, which
are concerned with distinctions rather than oppositions, with
the former being superior, morals and politics are expressed
as two distinctions. Politics is placed below morals, as
becomes evident in the final section of the passage.

Hegel, on the contrary, although accepting the existence of
the two systems, considers the political system hierarchically
superior, and finds in this superiority a very good argument
for the justification of the immoral behaviour of a politician.
This depends on whether that behaviour conforms to a superior rule. Provided, however, that should this superior rule be
incompatible with another rule belonging to the inferior
normative system, then the inferior rule must be considered
abrogated, and therefore invalid. I shall illustrate with the
usual pedagogic examples. If in the normative system of a
group of *latrones*, pirates, brigands, or even gypsies, not to
mention the mafia or the camorra so familiar to us, there is a
rule that considers theft lawful (naturally, of property not
belonging to the group members), it is obvious that the rule
prohibiting theft provided in the inferior normative system,
be it that of a state or church or of morals of those outside the
group, must be considered implicitly abrogated. This is simply because it is incompatible with a rule in the normative
system considered superior. Fundamentally, according to St
Augustine's famous maxim, even states could be *magna latro-
cinia* [great robberies].

Even more so, those who did not consider the state a
magnum latrocinium [great robbery] but 'a rational being in

and of itself', or the ultimate ethical moment and, by extension, the definitive phase of the objective Spirit (of practical
philosophy in the traditional sense of the word), should place
the state's imperatives over those dictated by personal morals. Hegel's system is a singular and highly illuminating example of the perfect inversion of the relation between morals
and politics, which had one of the highest expressions in
Kantian thought. This perspective is quite useful to illustrate
a form of justification of the immorality of politics that differs
from all those thus far examined. Hegel does not omit morals
in the traditional sense from the system, but they are considered an inferior phase in the development of the objective
Spirit, which finds its fulfilment in the collective morals or
ethicality (of which the state is the bearer).

Hegel was an admirer of Machiavelli, whom he praised in
his earlier work on the German constitution. A realist in
politics, Hegel knew the place for idle gossip when the hus-
sars come onto the field brandishing their shiny sabres.
Should the majesty of the state, 'of that rich framework
intrinsic to the ethos of the State', become subservient to
those who would counter it with 'the soft option of senti-
mentalism of friendship and imagination'?

In his *Philosophy of Right* (para. 337) Hegel summarizes the
relevant theory briefly but comprehensively. The paragraph
begins: 'At one time the opposition between morals and
politics, and the demand that the latter should conform to
the former, were much canvassed.' But Hegel intimates it is a
debate that has run its course, and is in fact anachronistic, at
least since we gained some understanding that the state's
welfare has a completely different 'justification' from the
wellbeing of individuals. The state has its objective reason
to exist, and only this physical existence counts as the principle for its action. It cannot rely on an abstract moral
imperative that leaves completely out of consideration the
needs and constraints dictated by the course of history.
According to this theory, the protagonist is the state, not
the single individual or even the sum of single individuals.
From this, among other things, derives the well-known thesis
that only universal History, rather than ahistorical morals

imposed on the state (by whom?), can judge the good or evil of states. This is because the fate of the world depends much more on their conduct than on the behaviour, moral as it might be, of any single individual. From this perspective, in my view, it is fair to say that for Hegel individual morals are inferior, as far as their validity is concerned, to the morals of the state. And when the state's historical process requires it, that validity must yield.

The end justifies the means

A dualist solution no longer only apparent but real is that transmitted historically with the term 'Machiavellian' because, rightly or wrongly, it is attributed to the author of *The Prince*. Here dualism is based on the distinction between two types of action. These are definitive actions that have an intrinsic value, and instrumental actions that are only valuable because they enable the attainment of a goal, which is regarded as having sole intrinsic value. Definitive actions, such as helping those who suffer and all the other traditional 'charitable acts' generally, are considered inherently good. These are judged for themselves, in that they are 'disinterested' actions, which are performed with no other ulterior motive than to accomplish a good deed. On the other hand, instrumental actions, or those that are good because of some other reason than themselves, are judged on the basis of their greater or lesser appropriateness to reach an aim.

There is no moral theory that does not observe this distinction. To illustrate with a well-known example, I refer to the corresponding Weberian distinction between rational actions consistent with a value (*wert-rational*), and rational actions consistent with an aim (*zweck-rational*). Likewise, there is no moral theory that does not recognize that an action can be judged in two different ways, according to the context in which it takes place, or according to the intention by which it was accomplished. To help the poor, an action usually cited as a typical example of a good action in itself, becomes a good action for other reasons, and must be judged as such, if it is performed with the aim of gaining merit. Nevertheless, if the action is performed without reward, it can also be said that the action was rational with respect to the value but certainly not with respect to the aim.

The basic core of Machiavellianism consists not so much of the recognition of the distinction between actions that are good for themselves and actions that are good for other reasons, but of the differentiation between morals and politics based on that distinction. It means, in short, that the sphere of politics is one of instrumental actions, and these should be judged not for themselves, but rather on the basis of their greater appropriateness to achieve the goal. This explains why, when referring to the Machiavellian solution, I spoke of the amorality of politics. Although the expression was never taken up (since it was unnecessary), it would correspond to the 'apolitical nature of morals'. What is meant by the amorality of politics is that politics overall represent a system of activities governed by rules, and judged according to certain rational criteria entirely different from morals. These also consist of a complex of actions, except that this system is governed by different rules and judged by different evaluative criteria. At this point the difference between the solution presently discussed and the previously analysed solutions becomes clearly evident. In the present solution the difference is based on the notion of detachment or independence between morals and politics, and as such it can easily and without attenuation be termed dualist. In the previous solutions, the difference is either a lack of separation, since politics is encompassed in the moral normative system, even if by a special measure, or a lack of independence, because morals and politics are in fact distinct but related through their interdependence. Thus the Machiavellian solution of the amorality of politics is presented as one whose fundamental principle is that 'the end justifies the means'. By contrast, we could define the non-political sphere (that governed by the divine entreaty) as the sphere where resorting to the distinction between means and ends is inappropriate, because every action must be considered for its intrinsic positive or negative value, regardless of the outcome.

With rigorist morals, such as the Kantian or those about duty generally, the consideration of an outcome external to the action is not only inappropriate but also impossible. This is because for the action to be moral, it must have no other aim than the fulfilment of duty itself, which is precisely the objective intrinsic to the action.

Even if the maxim 'the end justifies the means' is not literally attributable to Machiavelli, the passage in chapter XVIII of *The Prince* is usually considered its equivalent. There the question raised is whether the prince should keep his word (since the principle *pacta sunt servanda*, or pacts must be respected, is a universal moral principle regardless of whether its foundation is religious, rational, utilitarian, etc.). The reply reveals that those princes who achieved 'great things' had little regard for outcomes. It is clear from this passage that what counts in the behaviour of a statesman is the aim, or the 'great thing', and achieving the aim makes actions lawful, such as breaching agreements denounced by the moral code, which is the one that ordinary individuals must obey. It is not really clear in the passage just what constitute 'great things'. But one need not look far, since the first answer appears towards the end of the same chapter, where it states that what is important is for the prince 'to secure and preserve the state and his reputation'.

A second, clearer and more comprehensive, answer is that found in a passage of the *Discourses* (III, 41). There the theory of the separation is openly praised thus:

> If you are discussing nothing less than the safety of the home-land, then you should pay no attention to what is just or what is unjust, or to what is kind or cruel, or to what is praise-worthy or shameful. You should put every other considera-tion aside, and you should adopt wholeheartedly the policy most likely to save your homeland's life and preserve her liberty.

Nothing new under the sun, one might say. In this passage Machiavelli does no more than illustrate by articulating quite effectively the maxim *salus rei publicae suprema lex* (the high-est law is the security of the state). This is illustrated by contrasting the only principle, 'security of the state', that must guide political judgement with other possible criteria for judging human action. Based on the distinction between what is just and what is unjust, compassionate and cruel, commendable and contemptible, respectively, although from different perspectives, all these refer to common morals as the criteria of evaluation.

Two ethics

Among all the theories concerned with the relation between morals and politics, the one that has taken the thesis of separation to its extreme, and therefore can be regarded as most coherently dualist, acknowledges the existence of two sets of morals. These are based upon two different criteria for judging actions, and lead to evaluations of the same action that do not necessarily coincide. They are mutually incompatible, and cannot be superimposed upon each other. A classic example of the theory of the two types of morals is the Weberian notion of the distinction between the ethics of conviction and ethics of responsibility. What distinguishes these two sets of morals is precisely the different criterion adopted to judge an action good or bad. The first set of morals employs something that precedes action, be that a principle, a norm, or any other general prescriptive proposition. The function of any of these is to influence in a more or less determining manner the performance of an action, as well as allowing one to judge the concrete action either positively or negatively. This will depend on whether it complies or not with the abstract action intended by the norm. On the other hand, the second set of morals, which aims to provide a positive or negative judgement of an action, uses something that follows, or the outcome. As such, it provides a positive or negative judgement of the action based on whether the anticipated result is achieved or otherwise. Generally speaking, these two types of ethics can also be termed ethics of principles and ethics of results. In the history of moral philosophy they correspond, on the one side to deontological morals, such as the Kantian, and on the other to teleological morals, such as the utilitarian, which prevail today.

The two ethics, however, do not coincide. What is considered good based on principles may not mean the same based on results, and vice versa. When based on the principle 'Thou shalt not kill', the death penalty must be denounced. Conversely, based on the result, should it be proven that the death penalty can exert a significant power of intimidation, then it could be justified. In fact, abolitionists have striven to demonstrate, with the support of statistics, that it does have such a deterrent power.

This distinction traverses the whole history of moral philosophy regardless of the connection it may have with the distinction between morals and politics. This distinction becomes important when it is maintained that the ethics of a politician are exclusively ethics of responsibility (or of results). Moreover, a politician's action is judged on the basis of success or failure, and to judge it by using the criterion of loyalty to principles reveals abstract moralism, and therefore poor judgement in worldly affairs. Those who act according to principles are not concerned with the result of their actions. They do what they must, irrespective of the outcome. Conversely, those who are exclusively concerned with the result are not over-particular in complying with principles. They do what they believe is necessary regardless of what might happen. An example of the ethics of principles is illustrated by the judge who, as we often read in newspapers, asks a *pentito* [a terrorist or criminal who turns state's evidence] whether the group of terrorists had considered the question raised by the principle 'Do not kill'. The ethics of results, on the other hand, are depicted by the terrorist who replies that the only question the group would have considered was success or failure. If he has 'repented', it is not because he feels remorse for having violated the moral law, but because he accepts that ultimately their political action failed to achieve the proposed aims. In this sense, he cannot be considered a true repentant, but rather someone who realizes he made a mistake. He acknowledges neither guilt nor error.

It is possible for an aim not to be achieved, but it can also be possible that the aim attained may differ from the one proposed. During his trial, Archduke Ferdinand's assailant stated 'I did not expect that the assault would cause a war. I believed it would influence the younger generation towards nationalist ideas.' This was further supported by one of the accomplices who missed the target: 'The attempt produced unforeseen consequences. Had I been able to anticipate the outcome, I would have sat on the bomb and blown myself up.'

It is superfluous to dwell on the illustration of this well-known distinction, although it should be noted that the reduction of all politics to ethics of responsibility is an undue extension of Weber's thought. This is done despite the fact that on the subject of ethics and not meta-ethics, that is, of personal conviction rather than abstract theory, he is not at all prepared to effect this reduction. When considering the action of a great statesman, Weber argues that the ethics of conviction cannot be separated from the ethics of responsibility. The former of themselves and taken to their extreme consequences are characteristic of the fanatic, or of a morally repugnant figure. The latter, instead, disconnected from the principles that generate great things and completely aimed at success (as the Machiavellian expression 'provide us with a prince who will prevail' reminds us), characterize the figure of the cynic, which is morally no less reprehensible.

Is there a relationship between the different theories?

As a conclusion of this review of 'justifications', it is interesting to note finally, especially with regard to the last, which seems the most drastic, once one accepts the distinction between morals as ethics of conviction and politics as ethics of responsibility, how all five refer to each other. To this extent they can be considered variations, as may have already become apparent to the reader, of the same theme. Of course, this does not exclude the possibility, or negate the utility, of the distinction from the analytical point of view thus far adopted. In a descending scale, that is, by retracing our steps, the last variation, or the ethics of responsibility, is connected to the preceding variation, which consists of the Machiavellian doctrine. According to this, what matters in political decisions is the appropriateness of the means used to achieve the aim irrespective of the consideration of principles. The 'security of the state' is regarded as the ultimate aim of political action on which judgement of the goodness or otherwise of single actions depends, based on their greater or lesser compliance with the ultimate aim. This in turn refers directly to the preceding solution, which is provided by Hegel, who, as already stated, was an admirer of Machiavelli for whom the state (the 'homeland' in the *Discourses* and the *res publica* of the maxim inherited from traditional political morals) has its own 'objective' reason. This is the 'reason of state', or the term used by those political theorists who observe and comment on the creation and establishment of the modern state. That objective reason becomes the exclusive principle on which the ruler bases his action, and therefore of the positive or negative judgement that it can be given. On reflection, even the justification based on the specificity of professional ethics, or our second variation, derives from a clear preference for the aim as criterion of evaluation. What in fact characterizes a single profession is the common aim of all the group members, such as the health of the body for the doctor or of the soul for the priest. Among these specific professional aims, it is perfectly legitimate to list a third kind of health that is no less important than the other two: the *salus rei publicae*, as the aim inherent to the political leader. Finally, the first variation based on the derogation in case of necessity is, in my view, the most common, and it is the most common because all in all it is the least outrageous, or the most acceptable by whoever considers it from the viewpoint of common morals. Even this, however, can be interpreted as a deviation from the straight path, because in that particular circumstance pursuing such a course would lead to a destination different from that proposed or perhaps to no destination.

Accordingly, it might be worthwhile testing all these reasons for justification (and possibly others) by confronting a concrete historical case. One of these extreme cases is aptly depicted by the traditional figure of a tyrant, where the gap between the behaviour of an ordinary person, as morally prescribed, and the behaviour of a despot is more evident. One of these exemplars is the reign of Ivan the Terrible, a case that caused a most intense and passionate, now old, debate in both Russian and Soviet historiography.

I have chosen this case, although there are others just as appropriate, not only because it is truly an extreme example, but above all because a substantial scholarly synthesis by an historian quite sensitive to the issue under discussion is now available in an important text that has been translated into Italian.[6] All the reasons for justification analysed in this discussion are present in that text, in a more or less explicit form. This is especially the case for the first, or the state of necessity, and the last, or the result achieved. But all these *iustae causae* [just causes] are held together by the grandiosity of the aim, consisting precisely of Machiavelli's 'great things'. One of the historians considered, I.I. Smirnov, refers to the 'current necessity of the liquidation of the major representatives of the hostile aristocratic and boyar families'.[7] By this he means that necessity obeys no laws. There is an old saying which states that a person cannot be forced to do something impossible. By the same token, it follows that the same person cannot be prohibited from doing what is necessary. In the same way as the state of impossibility is incompatible with the observance of commands, the state of necessity is incompatible with the compliance of prohibitions. Hence, consideration of the state of necessity is closely connected to that of result. What makes an action a 'current necessity' is that it is considered the only possible condition for the achievement of the aim desired, and also considered 'good'. In fact, Smirnov inevitably concludes that despite the 'cruel form' this struggle for centralization took, that indeed was the price for progress and liberation from 'the impenetrable darkness of the forces of reaction and stagnation'.[8] But while we are discussing Ivan, our mind evokes Stalin. And Yanov in fact comments:

> If, in employing the same analogy, an historian were to main-
> tain that the Soviet Russia of the 1930s was truly steeped in
> betrayal, that all the ruling class was plotting against the state,
> that the peasants exploitation during collectivization and the
> loyalty of factory workers and clerks to their task was 'histor-
> ically necessary' for the survival of the state, he would also be
> forced to 'morally justify' all the terror and the Gulag.[9]

There is a final consideration. What all these justifications have in common is that they attribute the rules of political behaviour to the category of hypothetical norms. These can be in the form of conditional rules of the type 'if it is A, it must be B'. One such example is the case of the justification based on the relationship between rule and exception, or as in the form of technical or pragmatic rules of the type 'if you want A, you must do B', where A can be either only a possible or also a necessary aim, as in all the other cases. In any event, this exclusion of categorical imperatives from the sphere of politics conforms to the common view, according to which the behaviour of state leaders is guided by rules of prudence. These are understood as those rules that do not produce an unconditional obligation by leaving out of consideration both the situation and the aim. Rather, it is an obligation to be observed when that particular condition arises, or in order to achieve a specific aim. There is nothing more useful to clarify this essential feature of the moral theories of politics than an observation made by Kant, to whom we owe the first and most comprehensive elaboration of the distinction between categorical and hypothetical imperatives. If politics were to say: 'Be ye therefore wise as serpents', morality might add, by way of qualification: 'and harmless as doves'.[10]

Critical observations

Clearly, all these justifications (whatever their worth, but since they represent such a large part of modern political

philosophy they must have some value) do not aim to eliminate the moral question in politics. Rather, starting from the
importance of the problem, they propose to clarify the terms
and delimit its boundaries. I argued that one must justify the
deviation and not the rule. But the reason why it is precisely
the deviation that needs justification is because the rule
remains valid in all the instances where the deviation is not
justifiable. Despite all the justifications for a political behaviour that deviates from the rules of common morals, the
tyrant remains a tyrant. This is someone whose behaviour
cannot be justified by any of the theories, which even allow
for a certain normative autonomy of politics with respect to
morals. Although Machiavelli asserts that when the safety of
the homeland is at risk, no consideration must be given to
what may be 'kind or cruel', he denounces Agathocles as a
tyrant for 'ill using' his cruel actions. Bodin, described earlier
as an exceptional theorist of the state, provides a description
in some of his famous pages of the difference between a king
and a tyrant.

Let us briefly review the different theories:

1 State of necessity theory also holds that the reason why
   the exception confirms the rule is precisely because of the
   exception. Otherwise, were the criterion of the exception
   always valid, neither the exception nor the rule would
   survive. If a deviation can only be allowed if it is justified,
   it follows that it is presumed there are unjustifiable devia-
   tions and as such they are inadmissible.
2 Political ethics are those inherent to whoever undertakes
   political activity. However, political activity as conceived
   by those who argue from the perspective of professional
   ethics is not power of itself, but power to achieve an
   aim that represents the common good, or stated differently, the collective or general interest. It is not simply
   government, but good government. In fact, one of the
   traditional and persistent criteria on which to distinguish
   good from bad government is precisely the ability to
   judge whether this specific aim can be attained or not.
   Thus, it is good government if the common interest is

pursued and bad government if one's personal interest is pursued.

3 Are politics superior to morals? Such is not the case with all kinds of politics, but only the politics of those who at particular historical junctures realize the highest aim of the objective Spirit. These are the politics of the hero or the protagonist in our universal History.

4 The end justifies the means. But who justifies the end, or aim? Does not the end in turn also need to be justified? Is every end proposed by a state leader a good end? Should there be a further criterion that would allow one to distinguish good ends from bad ends? Should one perhaps ask whether bad means might even corrupt good ends?

5 Political ethics are the ethics of results, rather than of principles. But does this apply to all results? If one wants to differentiate between outcomes, is it not necessary, once again, to go back to principles? Can a good result be converted to immediate success? Are losers always in the wrong simply because they have been defeated? Could not today's losers be tomorrow's victors? *Victrix causa deis placuit/Sed victa Catoni*. Does not Caton belong to History? And so on.

The question of the legitimacy of the end

Although these questions do not represent an answer, they enable us to understand in which direction the answer should be sought. Such a direction is not that of the appropriateness of the means but of the legitimacy of the end. The two questions are not mutually exclusive, but since they are different it is worthwhile keeping them quite separate. The question of the appropriateness of the means is posed when a judgement on the efficiency of government is desired, which clearly is a technical rather than a moral judgement. Nevertheless, an efficient government is not of itself a good government. This further judgement is not satisfied by the attainment of the end, but also poses the question: what end? Having recognized that the end of political action is the security of the country, or the general interest or common good (contrasted with the ruler's security, particular interests, or personal benefit), that judgement, which is no longer on the appropriateness of the means but on the goodness of the end, is a real moral judgement. This is so, even if such a judgement, based on reasons attributed by all theories of justification, derives from morals different or partly different from common morals, according to which actions by single individuals are judged. This means that political action, as with every other human action that is free or presumed to be so, does not escape the judgement of whether it is right or wrong. One is mindful all the while of the specific reasons for political activity dictated by the so-called 'reason of state', which evokes the sinister episodes resulting from its improper use, even if the theory in itself indicates solely the distinctive features of political ethics. Clearly that moral judgement consists of what is right or wrong, and cannot be confused with the judgement of what is suitable or unsuitable.

The same question can also be posed in the following terms. Given that to a certain extent political activity concerns the attainment and preservation of power, or the highest power of one individual over another, ultimately the only power recognized is that of having the right to resort to force. (This is what distinguishes Alexander's power from that of the pirate who does not have this right.) Nevertheless, none of the justification theories illustrated here concerns the attainment, preservation, and expansion of power as good things in themselves. Moreover, none of them considers that the aim of 'immoral' political activity (morals compared with the morals of the *pater noster*, or as stated earlier of governing by divine entreaty) is only justified if it has 'great things', or 'the security of the homeland', as the end. To pursue power for its own sake would mean transforming a means, which as such must be judged in the same way as the aim, into an end itself. Even if one regards political activity as instrumental, it is not an instrument to be used by state leaders for any end they wish to pursue. Once the distinction between a good and bad end is accepted, a distinction informed by all the theories on the relation between morals and politics, it is inevitable that a good political action can be distinguished from a bad one. This, of course, means that it is submitted to a moral judgement. One example suffices. The debate on the moral issue often, and in Italy prevalently, concerns the subject of corruption in its manifold forms. These, in any event, are provided for in the penal code under the rubric of crimes, such as those of personal gain through official position, embezzlement, extortion, etc. More specifically, those that refer almost exclusively to party officials concern the subject of the so-called *tangenti* [substantial bribes that led to the *mani pulite*, or 'clean hands' trials]. One need only reflect briefly to realize that what makes every form of political corruption morally wrong (leaving aside its illegality), is the particular conduct of a politician who has become corrupt. This is based on the well-established presumption that he has placed his personal interest before the collective interest, personal benefit before the common good, or his and his family's welfare before the security of his country. In so doing, he fails in the duty of those who assume the task of political activity, and commits a politically improper action.

Our discussion could have ended at this point. However, in a state that upholds the rule of law, such as the Italian Republic, whose state of health prompted these reflections, a more inherently legal judgement on political activity, which goes beyond the evaluations of efficiency and of common or even political morals, is also warranted. Such legal judgement is concerned with compliance, or otherwise, with the fundamental rules of the Constitution. These are the rules that govern the practice of political activity, including that of the supreme organs of the state. Among the various established meanings of the state with the rule of law, I am referring to that which defines it as government by laws in contrast to government by men, and where government by laws is understood according to modern constitutionalism.

Judgement about varying levels of compliance by state organs, or by political parties as an integral part of sovereign power, with constitutional rules and the rule of law principles can give rise to a judgement of constitutional incorrectness and antidemocratic practice. Such a judgement frequently resounds in our current political debate. This occurs, for example, when there is an abuse of decree laws, or of the vote of confidence simply to put down the opposition. There is also, with regard to the parties, the practice of patronage that violates one of the fundamental principles of the rule of law, the visibility of power and the controllability of its exercise.

Often the political debate does not differentiate between the various judgements, and locates all three under the label of the 'moral question'. However, the three judgements – of efficiency, of legitimacy, and the more intrinsically moral (which could also be termed that of merit), on which I have dwelt exclusively – are distinct and must be kept separate for reasons of analytical clarity and attribution of responsibility.

Notes

1. See A. K. Sen, *On Ethics and Economics* (Oxford, Blackwell 1987), and 'Mercato e morale' ['The market and morals'], *Biblioteca della libertà* (1986), 94, pp. 8–27.
2. My reference is J. Burnham, *The Machiavellians: Defenders of Freedom* (New York, Putnam 1943).
3. B. Croce, 'L'onestà politica' ['Honesty in politics'], in *Etica e politica* [*Ethics and politics*] (Bari, Laterza 1945), p. 165.
4. J. Bodin, *Six Books of the Commonwealth*, (abridged and tr. M. J. Tooley (Oxford, Blackwell n.d.), p. 63.
5. Croce, 'L'onestà politica', p. 166.
6. A. Yanov, *The Origins of Autocracy* (Berkeley, University of California Press 1981).
7. Ibid., p. 307.
8. Ibid.
9. Ibid., p. 312.
10. H. Reiss, *Kant's Political Writings* (Cambridge, Cambridge University Press 1977), p. 116. Matthew X:16.

Reason of State and Democracy

The relation between morals and politics is one of the many aspects of the moral question, which today is livelier than ever. Among moral questions, the most traditional is that of the relation between morals and politics. Beside this there are also the questions of the relation between morals and private life, with particular emphasis on sexual relations, of the relation between morals and law, and of that between morals and art. Moreover, in the contemporary philosophical debate questions about the relations between morals and science, be they in physics or biology, are also emerging along with those between morals and technological development, and between morals and the economy (or, as it is often referred to, the world of business).

The fundamental problem, however, is always the same. It emerges from the realization that a contrast can occur between human activities in all these fields and some fundamental and fairly general rules of human behaviour. These are usually moral rules and as such are mandatory, simply because without them coexistence would be not only impossible, but also highly unsuccessful. To a certain extent, we can say that the aim of many moral rules is to enable a good coexistence. By the term 'good' 1 intend a kind of coexistence where mutually inflicted suffering between humans due to their behaviour has been reduced, and where some essential principles, such as liberty, justice, peace, and basic welfare,

are protected. This type of suffering, however, cannot be eliminated in the animal world, where the ruthless struggle for survival prevails.

The simplest, but least persuasive, way to resolve this problem is to maintain the autonomy between the different spheres of action and that regulated by moral prescriptions.

Let us consider the autonomy of art. Art has its own criterion of evaluation. This consists of what is beautiful or ugly, and is different to the criterion of right and wrong intrinsic to morals. The criterion by which science must be judged is whether something is true or false, which is also a different judgement from that of good and evil. In this same sense, in economics one speaks of the autonomy of market rules, which obey the utilitarian criterion. In the world of business one refers to the efficiency criterion that must exclude universal rules of conduct, which would render business transactions, if not impossible, more difficult to say the least, and less profitable.

One of the most controversial spheres is that of sexual relations. This is a particularly sensitive area, where every man or woman as such is affected and not only those in their professional capacity as artists, scientists, business people, etc. Autonomy in one's sexual life represents freedom in intimate relations with respect to prevailing morals. In other words, sexual relations do not have precise rules of behaviour or, simply put, they obey different rules to those of morals.

The same answer has been advanced for politics. This is what in the homeland of Machiavelli and Guicciardini was termed reason of state, or the autonomy of politics. The person who most successfully asserted this thesis was Carl Schmitt, who ascribed to the political sphere its own criterion of evaluation, which rests in the opposition 'friend–foe'. He stated: 'We assume that on the moral level the fundamental distinctions are right and wrong; on the aesthetic, beautiful and ugly; on the economic, useful and detrimental. The specific distinction that can encompass political actions and motives is the distinction between friend and foe.'

Although I have mentioned it in passing, it must be made quite clear that the analogy between the traditional distinctions of true–false, right–wrong, beautiful–ugly on the one hand, and friend–foe on the other, does not hold. They are oppositions located on two different levels, and cannot be placed after each other as if they belonged on the same level. Traditional dyads enable value judgements in the strict sense to be made. That is, one can express approval or disapproval of an action, and thus promote its consent or dissent. According to Carl Schmitt, the friend–foe dyad indicates the extreme level of intensity in a union or a separation, an association or a dissociation. But it does not express any value judgement that will allow the distinction between politically positive actions and politically negative actions, in the same way as, instead, the beautiful–ugly dyad does to distinguish between works of art that are to be aesthetically approved or disapproved. A friend is an ally, and a foe is someone to be fought. The contrast is not exhaustive, nevertheless, because between friend and foe there can be a neutral party, who is neither friend nor foe. If alongside the traditional dyads, we wanted to add a dyad that would allow value judgements on political behaviour to be made, we would have to resort to the dyad comprising what might be appropriate–inappropriate for the aim, or that of what is consistent–inconsistent with it. This, of course, is a criterion that can be used to provide a positive or negative judgement of a political action. It enables one to make a judgement of the action that is different both from the assessment of the useful–useless dyad by which one judges economic activity, and from the evaluation of the right–wrong dyad by which moral actions are judged. If one considers all the theories that support the autonomy of politics over morals, it becomes evident that they contrast the criterion of judgement of what is right or wrong with that of what is opportune or inopportune for a particular end. Hence, it is maintained that politics can be autonomous, because an action can be judged politically opportune even if it is not ethically right or economically useful. The Schmittian distinction of friend–foe is not really useful to characterize politics as an autonomous sphere with respect to values, but it can provide an explanatory definition of 'politics'.

The question of the relation between morals and politics emerges in the same way as it does in other spheres, where, to continue with our examples, there can be activities that are aesthetically valuable but morally deplorable, and actions that are economically useful but morally reproachable. I am thinking, to provide quite a contemporary example, of the problem of the sale of human organs. It has been argued that the best way to avoid the difficulty in finding kidneys for transplant is to consider them a commodity like any other. This is because there will always be some wretched person who, in order to repay debts or even simply to survive or, as has also been claimed, to secure a place to live, is prepared to sell one kidney. Furthermore, if in a market society the aim of business is profit, it cannot be excluded that profit will be pursued irrespective of the fundamental moral principle, which is respect for the person.

Analogously, the question of the relation between morals and politics can be posed in the following terms. It is commonly observed by anyone acquainted with history, past or present, that in the political sphere actions considered wrong by morals are continually performed or, conversely, actions that are right according to morals are neglected. It becomes evident from this observation that politics obey a code of rules that differs from the moral code. A few examples will demonstrate this.

The moral code, throughout the ages and in all countries, prescribes that we 'Do not kill'. History, however, can be objectively represented as an extended, continuous, and un-interrupted sequel of killings, slaughters of innocents, sense-less massacres, rebellions, revolts, bloody revolutions, and wars, which are usually justified by all kinds of argument. Hegel once remarked that human history is a 'huge slaughter-house'. It has rightly been noted that the precept 'Do not kill' is only valid within and not outside a group. In other words, it does not operate in relations between groups. This explana-tion renders the precept not to kill purely instrumental, and thus loses its characteristic of categorical imperative. It is valid within the group, because it ensures peace among its members, which is necessary for the group's survival. For the same reason, however, it is not valid outside the group, since this can only survive if it is capable of defending itself from the attack of hostile groups. But what am I saying? Is the authorization or obligation to kill the enemy part of the defence strategy?

The same reasoning can be applied to another fundamental precept of every set of morals, which is 'Do not lie'. There is a vast literature on the art of falsehood and concealment in politics. In *Crowds and Power*, Elias Canetti wrote some quite interesting passages on the topic. He states, 'Power is impenetrable. The man who has it sees through other men, but does not allow them to see through him. He must be more reticent than anyone; no-one must know his opinions or intentions.' He identifies Filippo Maria Visconti as an example of that impenetrability: 'He was unequalled in his capacity to disguise his thoughts.'[1]

Those with further interest can read Rosario Villari's *Elogio della dissimulazione*,[2] which, although referring only to the baroque age, provides examples and citations relevant to every age. Among the many citations, I select a passage by Justus Lipsius (1547–1606), who states: 'Should it displease some righteous person, he will cry out: "Let simulation and dissimulation be banished from human life". From private life, yes indeed, not so from the public, nor can it be done otherwise by whoever rules the whole Republic.' This is one of the many excerpts from which it seems one should be able to deduce that the distinction between morals and politics coincides with that between private and public. What currently are called morals would only be valid in private life. In public life other rules hold.

There is no political sphere free of conflicts. No one can expect to have the upper hand in a conflict without resorting to the art of pretence, deceit, or masking one's intentions. In the realm of perennial conflict for survival, such as nature, the different practices animals use to hide, burrow, and camouflage themselves are universal. Likewise, from the real duel or the ludic, which is fencing, to the technique of military strategy, the ability to pretend or 'the pretence' to deceive an opponent forms part of the conditions for success. Politics do not exist without the use of secrecy. Secrecy not only tolerates but also needs falsehood. To be bound by a secret means that one has the duty not to reveal it and the duty of non-disclosure implies the duty of falsehood.

A third example is the maxim on which any possible coexistence is founded, *pacta sunt servanda* [agreements are to be kept]. Every society consists of an interweaving of mutual relations. A society can survive while and until the assurance for that exchange of relations is guaranteed. This is the premise for one of the moral maxims that require the mutual observance of pacts. One of the examples provided by Kant that enables us to understand the meaning of the following fundamental ethical principle states: 'You cannot do what cannot become a universal maxim', which is precisely the observance of pacts. I must keep agreements because I do not want to live in a society where pacts are not observed. It would be a return to the state of nature where no one needs to observe a pact until he or she is equally certain that others will. But in the state of nature this certainty does not exist. Whoever observes pacts in a world where others do not feel obliged to observe them is destined to succumb.

Even this maxim does not appear to be as valid in public life as it is unconditionally in private life. It is usually observed that international treaties are useless pieces of paper. Commitments undertaken are only valid according to the formula *rebus sic stantibus* [in these circumstances]. International relations are based more on diffidence than on trust. A contractual society, instead, is a society based on trust. A society in which individuals distrust each other is a society where, since victory ultimately belongs to the strongest, everyone pursues security by force rather than wisdom.

This reference to wisdom confronts us with a further radical difference between the moral and political spheres, which encompasses them all. It is not by chance that the principal attribute of a politician is not so much knowledge or wisdom as prudence. This is the absolute ability to adapt principles to the solution of concrete situations. In the famous chapter XVIII of *The Prince*, Machiavelli states that a 'prudent' ruler is not obliged to keep his word when 'such

observance is detrimental to him'. The baroque-age beha-
viourist Balthazar Gracián wrote 'Serpents are masters of
every aspect of sagacity. They show us the path of prudence.'
Another attribute of the politician that closely follows prudence, and also of Greek derivation, is craftiness. This is no
longer represented by a serpent but by a fox. Craftiness, or in
Greek *metis*, goes back as far as Ulysses. Furthermore, in an
interesting book by Detienne and Vernant, one reads:

> *Metis* must foresee the unforeseeable. Committed to self-
> realization, prepared to confront new and ambiguous situ-
> ations, whose outcome is always certain, shrewd intelligence
> can influence human beings and issues, since it is able to
> foresee a more, or less, wide segment of the future beyond
> the immediate present. *Metis* appears as multiple, many-
> coloured, and shimmering. It possesses a duplicity that always
> enables it to be perceived differently than what it is, conceal-
> ing its lethal reality beneath reassuring appearances.[3]

Part of that craftiness to deceive the opponent is the inven-
tion of snares, traps, plots, ambushes, disguises, and diverse
stratagems (the Trojan horse being the most notable).

In an old Greek hunting and fishing treatise the two animals that best demonstrate *metis* are the fox and the octopus.
The fox's craftiness consists primarily of its ability to overturn
itself when an eagle attacks. The octopus's craftiness rests in
the multiplicity of forms it adopts to avoid capture. Craftiness in its human version is the *polútropos* figure, or the highly
resourceful individual. In recent years the study of metaphors, especially those based on animals, has become widespread in political language. One need only consider how
frequently in many political discussions the direct, or indirect, reference to 'hawks' and 'doves' is used. The metaphor of
the fox is best known. Less common, or perhaps neglected, is
that of the octopus. The octopus is capable of adapting to
diverse situations and can assume various aspects and impro-
vise numerous unexpected moves, which will make its action
more effective in a range of circumstances. It seems from this
depiction that today the same features are rather attributed to
a politician, derogatively called a 'chameleon'.

I would like to observe that none of these animal metaphors; serpent, fox, lion, octopus, or chameleon; could be used to depict a moral person who acts in the light of the universal good, and not only of the good of the city. This is yet another proof, if that were needed, of the irreducibility of the so-called political virtues, in the Machiavellian sense, to moral integrity.

At this point, having established that a divergence between moral rules and those of politics has always existed, and even persists today, two fundamental questions emerge. How can this divergence be explained? Is it right or wrong for such divergence to exist? While the former is a *quaestio facti* [question of fact], the latter is a *quaestio iuris* [question of justice]. Let us consider them respectively.

As stated at the outset, a plausible explanation certainly cannot be found in the thesis of the autonomy of politics with respect to morals. This thesis does not explain anything. Rather it is mere tautology. It is the same as saying that morals and politics are different because they are different. Yet the question of diversity is a serious one. This is because, although the historically verified and proven difference traverses our history, there is also the need for it to lapse, or failing this, for a good government to be one in which politics and morals tend to coincide. Perhaps alongside the realist theories, which hold that this difference cannot be eliminated, there are at least some idealist theories, which require politics to conform to morals, and if they fail to do that, they are bad politics.

In a well-known book, *The Corrupting Influence of Power*,[4] the German historian Gerhard Ritter maintains that the following two currents of thought were well represented at the beginning of the modern age. These are the realist current by Machiavelli, and the idealist by Thomas More, who describes the republican Utopia in which perfect peace rules with perfect justice. According to Ritter, moreover, the two currents of amoral and moral politics converged first in Hitler's Germany, and then in the Nuremberg trials against Nazi criminals and in the United Nations. It must not be forgotten that Machiavelli wrote *The Prince*, regarded as the unsurpassed example of realist politics, at the same time as Erasmus wrote *The Education of a Christian Prince*, which is considered a similarly perfect example of idealist politics.

In the history of political thought the contrast between realism and idealism recurs continually. There is no clearer example of this than the opposite positions adopted by two major philosophers of the modern age, Kant and Hegel, on the relation between morals and politics. Kant's ideal is the 'moral statesman'. This is the sovereign who interprets the principles of the art of politics in such a way as to coexist with moral principles. He upholds the maxim that organizational shortcomings must be corrected to conform to principles of natural law, 'even by the probable sacrifice of his particular interest'. Instead, Hegel accepts as valid the principle of the reason of state in its purest form. In his view, the principle according to which political morals, or what he terms 'ethic-ality', has priority over morals as such, or strictly speaking, private morals. From this follows the assertion according to which the existing contrast between politics and morals 'rests on the superficial way we depict morality, the nature of the state and its relations with the moral viewpoint'.

Despite the recurrent aspiration to reconcile politics and morals, in practice the contrast persists. One can easily understand why it gave rise to, and continues to motivate, endless attempts at explaining it. I will briefly outline three of them.

(1) The gap between morals and politics derives from the fact that political behaviour is guided by the maxim that the end justifies the means. The end, or goal, of politics is the preservation of the state or the public good. This common or collective good, or whatever term is used to refer to it, is considered so superior to the good of single individuals as to justify the violation of those fundamental moral rules, which apply to individuals and their mutual relations. Hence, the relevant traditional maxim: *salus rei publicae suprema lex* [the security of the state is the supreme law]. It would take far too long to raise the many weak aspects of this maxim. However, the moral criticism is primarily directed at the value of that

end. Not all the ends are so honourable as to justify the use of any means, which dictate the necessity for a government based on the rule of law as opposed to the rule of men. In such a government rulers govern according to established laws, are controlled by popular consent, and are responsible for the decisions they make. In the same passage where Machiavelli endorses the principle that the security of the homeland is the supreme good, in alluding to the king of France, he also states: 'Whatever his deliberation, the king must not suffer any shame, because irrespective of success or failure, whether he loses or wins, everyone will accept it as the king's prerogative.' Such an assertion is unacceptable in a state under the rule of law.

Moral criticism is also directed at the lawfulness of the means. Are all means lawful? Suffice it to think of all the rules that have progressively been established for what are now known as the laws of war, whose aim is essentially to limit the use of force. However, the fact that these limits are not respected does not mean that their violation is not perceived as a transgression against civil conscience. Even from this perspective there is a difference between a democratic and an undemocratic state. This applies to the use of more, or less, violent means by police as well as the exemplar of the abolition of the death penalty.

(2) The second justification is that prevalently provided by theories of the reason of state. According to these, politics must be subordinated to morals, except for some exceptional circumstances where a derogation of the principles is legitimate. No moral principle has absolute value; that is, none is valid without exceptions. Even the norm 'Do not kill' can in exceptional circumstances be violated. One of these circumstances is provided for in every penal code, and is legitimate defence. Another is the state of necessity, and because necessity has no law, it is a law in itself.

Since Carl Schmitt was cited at the outset, in this regard one cannot fail to recall that, in his view, the peculiarity of sovereignty rests in the power to decide when the condition of exception applies. Based on the principle of necessity, this is the condition that allows derogation of existing laws, or provisional suspension of their implementation.

Even under this aspect there is a difference between a democratic and non-democratic state. The Italian Constitution, for example, does not provide for the state of exception. It only provides for the state of war, but not for the state of necessity generally.

(3) The third justification is where the gap between morals and politics is linked back to the irremediable contrast between two forms of ethics, the ethics of principles and those of results (or consequences). The former judge action based on a pre-existent factor, such as the principle, maxim, or rule, 'Do not kill', 'Do not lie', or 'Observe established pacts'. The latter, instead, judge action based on the consequence or the effects of the action. While the two judgements may accord, more often they disagree. They would only accord if it were always true, which it is not, that observance of the principle yields good results, or that good outcomes are always and only achieved when observing principles.

I mention two examples. The first derives from a prohibitive norm, and the other from a permissive norm. Let us, once again, consider the prohibitive universal norm 'Do not kill'. Considered from the viewpoint of the ethics of principles, the death penalty should be abolished. However, if it can be demonstrated that the death sentence leads to some useful consequences in society, because it contributes to reducing the number of murders, in some exceptional circumstances it might be allowed. This, in any case, is the argument preferred by its supporters. Conversely, it could also be maintained that the death penalty conforms to the principle of retributive justice, according to which those who kill must be killed. On the other hand, the penalty must be abolished when, after taking the consequences into account, it can be demonstrated that it has no deterring effect for the majority of murders to which it is applied, and therefore becomes a needless cruelty. As we can see, the two judgements, either according to the principles or according to the consequences, differ in both cases. For the example of a permissive rule, I use the legislation on abortion now in force in many countries, including Italy. Based on the principle of 'Do not kill', there are sound arguments for abortion to be considered murder. Those who accept it, however, argue for its admission on the basis of the consequences as, for example, the inability to support the infant properly, or even excessive overpopulation, which humanity might no longer be able to confront with adequate resources.

What is the relation between the distinction of these two ethics and the distinction of morals and politics? The relation derives from the observation that in reality the distinction between morals and politics nearly always corresponds to the distinction between the ethics of principles and the ethics of results. In other words, a moral person acts and judges the actions of others according to the ethics of principles; a politician acts and judges the actions of others on the basis of the ethics of results. A moral person asks 'Which principles must I obey?' And the politician instead asks 'What consequences will follow from my action?' As I have stated elsewhere, a moralist may even accept the maxim *fiat iustitia pereat mundus* [let there be justice even if the world perishes], but a politician's actions are of this world and in support of it. He cannot make a decision as a consequence of which 'the world will perish'.

The first explanation, 'the end justifies the means', is based on the distinction between categorical and hypothetical imperatives. It only allows hypothetical imperatives: 'If you want, you must.' The second explanation, based on derogation, rests on the distinction between the general rule and the exceptional rule. The third and final explanation, which contrasts the ethics of principles with those of responsibility, goes even further and discerns that the judgement over the approval or disapproval of our actions becomes divided. Thus, two different moral systems emerge, whose judgements do not necessarily coincide. It is from this division that the antinomies in our moral life emerge. These antinomies, or contradictions, in turn create those particular situations that we all experience almost daily, and are referred to as 'cases of conscience'.

The realization that morals and politics are separate does not preclude the fact that there are different levels of diversification. Nevertheless, even if the perfect solution of politics through morals is impossible, it is still desirable to have a situation where the gap is reduced.

I have repeatedly contrasted democracy with non-democratic regimes. I argue, in fact, that one of the positive characteristics of democracy that enables us to say that it is the best, or less evil, among forms of government, is also this: democracy is the political system that allows for the closest encounter between the needs of morals and those of politics.

I recall the observations made at the outset, where to underscore the gap between morals and politics I provided the three examples 'Do not kill', 'Do not lie', and 'Pacts must be observed'.

In summary then, I state as follows:

1   Democracy is that form of government whose principal rules, when observed, have as their aim the solution of social conflicts without the need to resort to mutual violence (heads are counted, not severed).
2   In order to exist and grow stronger, democracy needs the broadest extension in the relation of mutual trust between citizens, and therefore must banish the strategy of falsehood and deceit as much as possible (likewise reducing the space for secrecy).
3   Since democracy presupposes and requires a pluralistic society where different power groups compete peacefully in making collective decisions, it is a regime where the greater number of decisions is made by agreements between the different groups. Thus, democracy creates a highly contractual society, which as such presupposes and requires observance of the maxim *pacta sunt servanda*.

It is not anticipated that the gap between the needs of morals and those of politics will be completely eliminated. It is expected that politics, however, might respect the moral ideal of a good society more in a democracy than in any of the different forms of despotic government that have raged in the world, and are still present today. Understandably, not all democracies are the same. But it is precisely the different relation between morals and politics, which I have briefly illustrated, that should enable us to identify good democracies from bad, and the better from the worse democracies. Thus, it would also indicate the direction we must take to enable the democratic form of government to become progressively closer to its ideal.

I have often spoken about the unkept promises of democracy. A good criterion on which to measure the distance between the ideal and the real is the consideration of the relation between morals and politics. We can judge what level of political violence exists from time to time in historical democracy, and to what extent political relations are still covered by secrecy (which, as stated, encourages the practice of falsehood). Finally, that criterion enables us to judge how strong the binding agreements between social and political forces are, because from these derives the greater or lesser effectiveness of a pluralist society, such as the democratic is.

Notes

1. E. Canetti, *Crowds and Power* (London, Gollancz 1962), p. 292.
2. R. Villari, *Elogio della dissimulazione: La lotta politica nel Seicento* [*In Praise of Dissimulation: Political Struggle in the Seventeenth Century*] (Bari, Laterza 1987).
3. M. Detienne and J.P. Vernant, *Cunning Intelligence in Greek Culture and Society* (Hassocks, Harvester Press 1978), pp. 20–1.
4. G. Ritter, *The Corrupting Influence of Power* (Tower Bridge, Hadleigh 1952).

Part II

The Nature of Prejudice

What is prejudice?

By 'prejudice' is understood an opinion or a range of opinions, sometimes even an entire doctrine, which is received uncritically and passively by tradition, custom, or an authority whose dictates are accepted without question. We accept such authority 'uncritically and passively' without verifying it, out of either inertia, respect, or even fear. We accept it with such firm conviction as to resist any rational confutation; that is to say, rejecting any rebuttal that resorts to rational arguments. This is why it can be quite correctly stated that prejudice falls within the sphere of the non-rational, or is among those beliefs which do not emerge out of reasoning and thus evade any confutation based on argument.

The fact that prejudice belongs to the sphere of ideas refractory to reason serves to distinguish it from any other type of erroneous view. Prejudice is a false view that is strongly believed to be true, but not every ill-founded view can be considered a prejudice. A simple example is the type of error any one of us can make when learning a foreign language. These errors, however, do not derive from a prejudice, but emerge out of our ignorance of certain rules of that language. What is the difference between this kind of error and that caused by prejudice? The difference lies in the fact that the error we make in writing in a language we do not know well is one that can be corrected once our knowledge

increases. In other words, we engage with subjects that challenge our reasoning ability and learn by experience.

Another type of error that cannot be confused with prejudice is the error we encounter when we are deceived into
believing that something is true, and instead it is not.
Although we can make an error in good faith, even in this
case, once the deceit is discovered, we are able to acknowledge the error and restore the truth. Generally, one can say
that it is possible to distinguish an erroneous view, such as
prejudice, from all those views that can be corrected by
reason and experience. Precisely because it does not allow
for correction or is less easily corrected, prejudice is a more
persistent as well as a socially more dangerous error.

We may now ask ourselves why prejudice, more than any
other error, is so strong as to resist rational argument. The
following view could be advanced. The strength of prejudice
usually derives from the fact that we want to believe as true a
false opinion, since it meets our wishes, stimulates our passions, and serves our interests. However, behind that conviction that enables us to believe what prejudice tells us we
should believe, there is a practical reason. A consequence of
this practical reason, therefore, is also a propensity to believe
the view transmitted by prejudice. This propensity to
believe can be termed a bias. Prejudice and bias are usually
interconnected. Prejudice can be grounded more easily in
those who are already favourably predisposed or have a bias
towards accepting it. For this reason, prejudice as an erroneous view that is strongly believed to be true can be distinguished from all other kinds of error, because usually these
have no bias. And because they have no bias, they can be
more easily corrected.

Different forms of prejudice

There are different forms of prejudice. An initial useful distinction is that between individual and collective prejudices.
In this discussion I will not deal with individual prejudices,
such as superstitions, which are largely idiotic beliefs relating

to the evil eye, jinx, and hex. These beliefs induce some people to carry a horn-shaped charm as protection, or to gesticulate in peculiar ways to exorcise a danger, or to avoid activities that involve travelling on Fridays, or seating at a dinner table in a group of thirteen. They may even acquire amulets to repel misfortune or talismans to attract it. I am not really concerned with these, since they are generally harmless, or at least they are not in any way as socially threatening as collective prejudices.

I term 'collective' those prejudices which are shared by one social group with respect to another social group. The danger of collective prejudices derives from the fact that many conflicts between groups, which can also degenerate into violence, are caused by the distorted way one social group judges the other, resulting in misunderstanding, rivalry, hostility, contempt, or derision. Usually such distorted judgement is reciprocal. The more intense the identification by individual members is with their group, the stronger the judgement. Identification with one's group makes the other individuals seem different, or even hostile. Hence prejudice, or the negative judgement which the group members make about the inherent characteristics of the rival group, contributes to the establishment of either identification or contrast.

There are all kinds of group prejudice. However, the two most historically significant and influential are national prejudice and class prejudice. It follows that the important conflicts that marked the overall history of humanity are those caused by wars between nations or peoples (or even races) and class struggles. There is no nation that does not have behind it a persistent, unswerving, and seldom modifiable idea of its identity, which rests on its claimed and presumed diversity from all the other nations. There is a big difference between the way in which a population perceives itself, in the face of opposition, and the way it is seen by other populations. But both ways usually derive from rigid ideas and superficial generalizations, such as that all Germans are arrogant, or that all Italians are crafty, etc., which is why they are termed 'stereotypes'. To provide a more familiar example, I can think of the view Piedmontese people hold of themselves (which is a positive idea), and of the view other Italian regions usually have of them (which is the exact opposite). Again, both of these are stereotypes. It is stereotypical to say that Piedmontese are good workers, are well behaved, and do not engage in idle talk. The same applies for the stereotype that they are sloggers, slow-witted, and interpersonally cold.

It is superfluous to say any more on the existence of class prejudice, since it is a fact of common experience. There is no need to explain that class conflict also, but not only, emerges from prejudice. It is caused by the real contrast between the 'haves' and the 'have nots', between the exclusive proprietors of the means of production and those who have no other possessions than the potential value of their labour. But there is no doubt that any contrast is reinforced by prejudice, which results in the negative way these two opposing classes describe each other.

Prejudice and discrimination

I will deal with prejudice in terms of its harmful consequences. The main consequence of group prejudice is discrimination. From the previous examples of national (or regional) prejudice and class prejudice, to which we must add racial prejudice, it can be derived that the main consequence of collective prejudice is the distinction, or rather the contrast, between groups that discriminate against each other.

What do we mean by discrimination? The term is relatively new and was introduced and diffused, above all, in connection with the racial campaigns, first the Nazi and subsequently the fascist, against Jews who, compared with the dominant group, were considered a 'discriminated' group. Discrimination, however, means more than difference or distinction, because it is always used with a pejorative connotation. In short, 'discrimination' can mean an unjust or illegitimate differentiation. Why is it unjust or illegitimate? It is so because it violates the fundamental principle of justice (which philosophers term 'distributive justice') according to which all individuals who are the same must be treated equally. Discrimination can be seen to occur when those who on the basis of criteria commonly accepted in civilized countries (for example, those prescribed by article 3 of the Italian Constitution) should be treated the same, but are not.

Let us try to get a better understanding of discrimination by identifying its different phases. Initially, discrimination is based on a superficial judgement, or on the observation that there are differences between humans, and between groups. There is nothing reproachable in this type of factual judgement: humans are *in fact* different from each other. But even the realization that humans are not the same does not quite produce a discriminating judgement.

A discriminating judgement needs another type of judgement, and this is not one of fact but of value. In other words, in judging the two different groups, one is considered good and the other bad, or one is regarded as civilized and the other barbarian, or one superior (in intellectual ability, moral virtues, etc.) and the other inferior. Accordingly, it is one thing to say two individuals or two groups are different, which is simply a mere factual observation that can be based on objective data. It is another to say that the former is superior to the latter. Such a judgement introduces a criterion of distinction, which is no longer factual but evaluative. As with all value judgements, this judgement is historically relative, or even subjectively conditioned. This confusion between factual and value judgements occurs regularly in racial discrimination, which is one of the most hideous. The fact that blacks are different to whites is simply a factual judgement. Among other things, it is such an obvious difference that it is undeniable. Discrimination begins when we go beyond observing that blacks are different, and add that whites belong to a superior race and blacks to an inferior race. But they are inferior in relation to what? To be able to state that one human is superior to another, one must have an evaluative criterion. But how is such a criterion derived? Usually one is concerned with a criterion that is uncritically transmitted within a certain group. As such it is upheld by the strength of tradition or based upon an acknowledged authority, for example, on a text considered infallible by its followers, such as Hitler's *Mein Kampf.*

The process of discrimination does not stop here, but concludes in a third and decisive phase. In order for discrimination to reveal all its negative consequences, it is not sufficient for a group to assert, on the basis of a value judgement, its superiority over the other. One can accept that there are individuals who consider themselves superior to others, but this judgement does not necessarily imply the consequence that it is their duty to enslave, exploit, or even kill them. Let us consider the common relation between parents and children. One does not take exception to the factual judgement according to which parents are different (in age, experience, strength, etc.) to their children. Similarly, one does not object to the consideration of parents' superiority over their children, since this superiority can be partly based on objective reasons, at least while the children are minors. The consequence that follows from these two judgements is not that the superior party must suppress the inferior. Rather, what happens in familial relations is precisely the opposite, in that the parent, as the superior party, must help the child. To provide a contemporary example, the same happens in relations at the global level between North and South. No one doubts the superiority, at least from a technological perspective, of the North over the South. However, no one can maintain that as a consequence of such superiority it is acceptable for those in the North to live in abundance while those in the South die of starvation. Relations of diversity and superiority do not imply the consequences of racial discrimination. This does not stop at the consideration of the superiority of one race over the other, but makes a further decisive step (which I identified as the third phase in the discrimination process). According to this, it is precisely on the basis of the judgement that one race is superior and another inferior that the former must command and the latter must obey, the first must dominate and the other be subject, and finally the former should survive and the other must die. From the relation of superiority and inferiority two different conceptions can emerge. According to the first conception, the superior party has the duty to help the inferior party to reach a higher level of wellbeing and civilization. According to the second conception, the superior has the right to suppress the inferior. It is only when diversity leads to the second way of conceiving the relation between superior and inferior that we can appropriately speak of real discrimination with all the aberrations that follow from it. Among these aberrations, the most destructive in our history was the 'final solution', conceived by the Nazis to resolve the Jewish question in the world. This consisted of the systematic extermination of all Jews, who lived in all those countries dominated by Nazism. To reach this conclusion, the Nazi regime underwent three different phases of judgement: (1) Jews are different to Aryans; (2) Aryans are a superior race; (3) superior races must dominate and, should it be necessary for their preservation, even eliminate the inferior races.

The different types of discrimination . . .

So far I have drawn our major example of discrimination from the racial type. But this is not the only one.

There are many others. As mentioned, article 3 of the Italian Constitution states: 'All citizens have equal social status, and are equal before the law.' The affirmation that all citizens are equal is already of itself a standpoint against any form of discrimination. In fact, as I have already stated, discrimination rests first of all on the idea that humans are unequal. The article continues: 'without distinction of sex, race, language, religion, political views, personal and social conditions'. I dwell in particular on the discrimination due to political views and on that due to personal and social conditions. The former becomes increasingly more irrelevant, at least in a democratic state that is pluralistic in its nature and survives because of such pluralism. Even if it is not completely true that following one political view instead of another does not have practical consequences it is, however, accepted in principle, and no longer debatable, that in a democratic society everyone is free to follow the political view they think best. To provide an example of discrimination for one's political views even in a democratic state, we can recall the *Berufsverbot* that was in force in the German Federal Republic. This was a provision that excluded adherents to certain movements or political parties considered subversive from attaining certain public office positions. One of the primary objectives of the workers' statute in force in Italy from 1970 was to guarantee freedom of opinion even in the factory. In fact, article 1 states that workers 'have the right in their workplaces to express their opinions freely'.

With regard to the personal and social conditions there is a need first of all to interpret the exact meaning of this expression. It can be noted in rather general terms that there are certainly some impairments that fall within personal conditions, such as those that today characterize the commonly referred-to category of the 'handicapped'. Among the social conditions there is the one which describes one's belonging to a social class. As far as our discussion is concerned, suffice to say that the problem of a possible (not only possible, but also actual) discrimination of the handicapped exists and is continuously debated, especially in education policy. This does not take into consideration, say, the discrimination based on the distinction of social class. Despite the language in article 3 of the Italian Constitution, such discrimination persists in many situations, such as in the application of criminal law, which notwithstanding the principle inscribed on the gables of every law court, 'The law is the same for all', is often more sympathetic and less rigid towards the rich and powerful.

... And their differences

After listing the most common forms of discrimination, we need to see whether we can identify some important differences between them. We have already stated that discrimination rests on the observation of a difference or an inequality between individuals, and between groups. Now the major distinction that we wish to make between different forms of inequality is the distinction between natural and social inequalities. This distinction is relative rather than absolute. But in certain respects this is a distinction that has a basis. Everyone can see that the difference between a man and a woman is a natural difference, whereas linguistic difference is a social or historical difference. This is demonstrated by the fact that while a man cannot be transformed into a woman and vice versa (except in special cases), a man or a woman can speak in two or more different languages. It is also possible that they may have spoken various languages during different periods of their lives.

The distinction between these two types of inequality has been of considerable importance throughout the history of political thought. One of the constant human aspirations is to live in a society of equals. But clearly natural inequalities are a great deal more difficult to remedy than the social. For this reason, those who resist the demands for greater equality tend to maintain that the greater number of inequalities are natural, and as such are insuperable or more difficult to eliminate. Conversely, those who struggle for a greater equality are persuaded that by far the greater number of inequalities are social or historical. Suffice it to recall Rousseau, the prince of egalitarian writers, who maintains in the *Discourse upon the Origin and Foundation of the Inequality Among Mankind* that nature created men equal, but civilization rendered them unequal. In other words, he argues that inequalities between humans have a social origin, and it follows that by returning to nature they can regain equality. Now let us for a moment consider the prince of inegalitarian writers, (the anti-Rousseauan) Nietzsche, and author of *Beyond Good and Evil*. For him, humans are unequal by nature, and only society with its morals adapted to suit the herd, its religion of compassion for the misfit, has rendered them equal. While Rousseau considers inequalities artificial and therefore to be condemned and eliminated, Nietzsche regards them as natural, and therefore neither to be condemned nor surmounted. Hence, an advocate of egalitarianism condemns social inequalities in the name of natural equality, and conversely, in the name of natural inequality, a supporter of inegalitarianism condemns social equality.

The difference between natural inequality and social inequality is important for the question of prejudice for the following reason. Often prejudice emerges from the superimposition of a social inequality on a natural inequality, without recognizing it as such. Furthermore, by not recognizing that the natural inequality has been aggravated by the superimposition of an inequality created by society, and because it is not being recognized as such, it is considered ineliminable. This is precisely what occurred in the feminist question. The natural differences between men and women are obvious. But the condition of women that feminist movements reject is that in which social and historical differences have been added to the natural difference. Those are the differences that cannot be justified as being natural, and since they are artificially produced by a society upheld by males, they can (or must) be eliminated. Another natural difference is that between a mentally healthy person and a mentally ill person. But certain social discriminations produced by prejudices have been superimposed on the natural difference. Today, one of the most debated examples of the distortion of a natural difference through a social prejudice is that which concerns homosexuals. Even in this case one can speak of a natural difference between homosexuals and heterosexuals. However, the negative judgement that in our society is given to homosexuality has an historical origin. This is supported by the fact that among the educated class in ancient Greece, such a negative judgement did not exist. Rather, the love of wise older men for young men was considered superior to heterosexual love.

Among the forms of discrimination we are discussing, the linguistic and those that derive from adherence to a particular religion instead of another are more of a social than natural kind. Religion, like language, is a social product. This is demonstrated by the fact that while natural inequalities cannot be removed, it is not inconceivable that linguistic and religious differences can be eliminated. In the same way as the ideal of a universal religion has always existed, the proposal for a universal language has similarly often been advanced. A universal religion is one that is the same for everyone, in the same way as a universal language is one that is the same for all. While it is unlikely that race difference will disappear, since it is a difference that does not depend on the will of humans, differences between languages and religions could one day disappear, if we could manage to establish a general agreement to unify the two.

Of course, irrespective of its legitimacy, the difference between natural and social inequalities must be considered with great caution. But it serves to make us understand that prejudice is a social phenomenon, and the product of the mindset of groups historically formed, which precisely because it is such can be eliminated.

Prejudice and minorities

There is one final observation. It has been stated that collective prejudice, the type I have been exclusively concerned with, is the attitude adopted by a group in respect of individuals of another group. It can be added that the group against which a hostile prejudice is formed is nearly always a minority. Group prejudice is generally a prejudice of the majority against a minority. In this sense, racial prejudice is typical. Victims of group prejudice are usually ethnic, religious, and linguistic minorities, etc. In fact, the attitude of Catholics towards Protestants or Jews in general is one thing. It is another to have the same attitude when Protestants, as in the case of the Waldensians in Piedmont in ancient times [1686] now fortunately over,[1] or when Jews, as was for centuries the case of the establishment of ghettoes, represent a minority among the majority. The same can be said for the prejudice of Italians in the north against southern Italians. This became even stronger, following the emigration phenomenon, as greater numbers coming from the south formed a minority group living within the majority. The case of linguistic minorities is also similar. There is generally no prejudice against those who speak a different language. But prejudice can emerge when those who speak differently represent a restricted pocket in a larger environment, which naturally aims to have its language prevail over that of the minority.

While it may be true that group prejudice usually affects minorities, there is at least one exception that must cause reflection. The series of prejudices held by men against women does not concern a minority, since the number of women is more or less the same as that of men, and they do not live separately in minority groups. I reiterate that there are natural inequalities between men and women, which it would be silly to ignore. But it is a fact that several of the inequalities between the conditions of men and women have social origins, so that their relations change according to different societies. The emancipation of women, which we have been witnessing for years, is an emancipation that must also advance through the critique of many prejudices. In other words, it must eradicate those entrenched mental attitudes that are grounded in customs, ideologies, literature, and the way people think. Because they are so entrenched the notion of their origin has been forgotten and those who continue to adopt them in good faith believe they are judgements based on facts.

Precisely because these prejudices that have intervened between men and women concern half of humanity and not only small minorities, one may consider that the movement for the emancipation of women and their attainment of equal rights and conditions is the most significant (I would be tempted to go so far as saying that it is the only) revolution of our time.

The consequences of prejudice

I started from the premise that prejudice must be fought because of its consequences. But what are these consequences? The harmful consequences of prejudice can be arranged on three different levels, which I differentiate according to the degree of severity or intensity.

We begin from legal discrimination. There is a principle in modern legislations according to which 'all are equal before the law'. This principle means that everyone should enjoy the same rights. One of the effects of discrimination is that some individuals are excluded from the enjoyment of certain rights. Since earlier we discussed the feminist question, here we are aided by a rather simple and illuminating example. In Italy, women were excluded from voting until 1946; that is, they could not enjoy the same right as men. It was a real discrimination, even if it was not always regarded as such. The consequence of such discrimination was, of course, impairment. During the last years of the fascist regime, when the campaign against the Jews broke out in Italy as well, the initial consequence was the deprivation inflicted upon those who were considered to belong to the Jewish race of certain rights, which they enjoyed before the racial discrimination in the same way as all other Italians. In this case also, there was a group that was no longer the same as the others for certain rights.

A second, and rather more serious, consequence of discrimination is social marginalization. The classic example in the Christian world is the ghetto where for centuries Jews were relegated. Although they are not institutionalized, there are ghettoes for ethnic or social minorities in all the big cities. Suffice to think of the black neighbourhoods in American cities such as Harlem, or the shantytowns that surround certain major capitals. The extreme form of marginalization is that practised in so-called closed institutions, such as prisons and mental asylums. Even in this case, the process of emancipation coincides with the recognition of discrimination, which often results from being aware of prejudice. With regard to the relation between the sexes, even if in a polemical form, often the home to which a woman was for centuries relegated today is compared to a kind of ghetto. This marked the social marginalization of women, both physically and spatially.

The third and most serious phase of the process of discrimination is political persecution. Here what I mean by political persecution is the use even of force to suppress a minority of 'unequals'. This third phase represents, quite dramatically, the extermination of the Jews and of other minorities, such as gypsies, perpetrated by the Nazi regime.

A sketched conclusion

I am well aware that I should be concluding by answering the question: 'But if prejudice produces so much harm to humanity, is it not possible to eliminate it?' Quite frankly, I unfortunately have to acknowledge my inability to provide an answer to such a question. Those who know a little history are aware that there have always been evil prejudices, and even when some of these are eliminated, others will immediately emerge.

I can only say that prejudices originate in the mind, and it is there that they must be fought. This can be done through the development of knowledge, and therefore through education and the relentless struggle against every form of sectarianism. There are men who kill each other over a game of football. Where does this passion start other than in their minds? Although it is not a panacea, I believe that democracy can be used even for this. By democracy I mean a society where opinions are free and therefore bound to clash, and through this process they become refined. For humans to be able to free themselves of prejudices, they first of all need to live in a free society.

Note

1. [Translator's note: Waldensians were members of a reforming body of Christians, followers of Peter Waldo (Valdo) of Lyons, and formed about 1170. Their chief seats were in the Alpine valleys of Piedmont, Dauphiné, and Provence. The Waldenses joined the Reformation movement, and were often severely persecuted, especially in the sixteenth and seventeenth centuries.]

Racism Today

Racism has become one of the major problems of our time, and will be increasingly more so in the foreseeable future. Italians have always been a population of emigrants. It is only in recent years that Italy has become an immigration destination, and we should not be under any illusion that this trend will not increase. Following the collapse of communism, immigration from Eastern European states is supplementing that of countries which we conventionally call the Third World. When compared to the types of immigration of the last century, the severity of the current problem rests in the fact that the immigration flow then derived from overpopulated countries, such as Italy, towards populated countries, such as the Americas, or those sparsely populated, such as Australia. Today, quite the opposite is happening. Immigration flows into European countries, which are already among the most populated in the world.

Confronted with mass immigration, the problems a country such as Italy must face are quite different from those encountered, for example, by Australia. Among these, there is the rise of racist phenomena. The population of a host country must suddenly and unpredictably be able to coexist with other individuals with different and sometimes unknown customs, let alone the language, and often the only attempt to communicate is by signs or garbled sentences. This situation inevitably generates, and I stress 'inevitably', certain diffident attitudes, which may range from verbal mockery to rejecting any form of communication or contact, or from segregation to aggressiveness.

'Are Italians racist?' This is the persisting question for which some answers have been sought even through polls and surveys. I will simply mention one survey that was undertaken in Turin, curiously titled *Rumore* [*Noise*]. It concludes that for now the racist attitude is only a background noise, which has not yet translated into actions, and seldom surfaces to the point of creating a social disturbance. The book's contents are revealed by its subtitle, *Attitudes Towards Foreign Immigrants*. It begins with the chapter, 'Ethnic prejudice and its different forms of expression'. Prejudice is then identified according to the characteristic it assumes, either general or particular. The particular is in turn classified into socio-cultural, socio-economic, and personal.

I provide some examples that demonstrate there are no surprises: prejudice is monotonous. The expressions that are currently employed to address the *extra-comunitari* [migrants from non-European-Union countries] are largely the same as those used in addressing southern Italians a few decades ago here in Turin. The general type of prejudice would posit that 'they have more defects than merits and invade our territory'. The socio-cultural type of prejudice instead might argue that 'they seem different in their mentality, behaviour, social life, and traditions'. According to socio-economic prejudice, 'they are loafers, they expect our support and threaten our interests'. Finally, a personal kind of prejudice would say that 'they are ill-bred, dishonest, dirty, carriers of contagious diseases, violent with women, etc.'.[1]

Ethnic prejudice is one of the many types of prejudice that riddle our minds, and one of the most dangerous, also because it is difficult to eradicate. Pierre-André Taguieff's *La force du préjugé*, a book, in my view, less cited than it deserves, is a kind of general compendium on the nature and various forms of prejudice. The volume contains more than six hundred pages, and as we learn from its subtitle, *Essai sur le racisme et ses doubles*, is predominantly devoted to racial prejudice.[2] Prejudice is defined as a 'premature judgement'. This attitude leads one to 'think one knows without actually knowing, to predict without sufficient and clear evidence, and to draw conclusions without possessing the necessary certainties'. Thus prejudice not only generates erroneous opinions, but unlike the usually incorrect opinions it is much more difficult to eradicate. This is because the error derives from an irrational belief and not from an incorrect reasoning that can prove to be false. Nor does it derive from the assumption of a fact whose falsity can be empirically proven.

The 'reasons for racism'

To emulate a saying, those without prejudices may cast the first stone. We must be cautious in rejecting the prejudices of others. Often we contrast one prejudice with another. In other words, we oppose a falsely believed incorrect view with an emotionally assumed incorrect view. We may state, for example, that all humans are the same (which is not true), or supported by scientific claims we might argue that there are no different groups, which can be called 'races' without necessarily deriving from them hostile attitudes. I would conclude that there is no worse prejudice than that of believing we have no prejudices. As Montesquieu stated, 'I call prejudice not only that which enables certain issues to be ignored, but above all that which allows us to ignore ourselves.'[3] There is nothing more irritating than prejudicial antiracism, which refuses to take into account the real reasons for racism. To paraphrase an assertion by Leonardo Sciascia, which has become famous for unfortunate reasons, I would suggest one be wary of antiracist experts. My concern is to try and understand racism before condemning it. It is far too simple to do this, since being racist is so infamous that no one would declare it publicly (this is the reason why opinion polls are not always very reliable). Instead, one needs to understand it, because, if by 'racism' one means an initial superficial attitude of distrust towards someone who is different, especially if subsequently that individual unexpectedly interferes with our life, there is an element of racism in each of us. Thus there is nothing worse than cheap moralism because usually when it is cheap it is also hypocritical. Moreover, and above all, it is only when we try to understand the reasons for racism that we can attempt to correct it, and ultimately eliminate it.

Racism is not something that just happens. It is not an attitude that manifests itself outside certain circumstances. One is not generally or abstractly racist towards all individuals who are different. We can exhibit indifferent attitudes, and sometimes also those of empathy or admiration, towards certain groups of persons who are different. A preliminary condition for a racist attitude or behaviour to develop is our coming in direct contact with another person or, more specifically, several persons. This is because racism is not directed so much at a single person, for whom one can exhibit feelings of hatred, contempt, or general aversion, but at a group, or more precisely at single individuals because they belong to a particular group. The factual and most persistent form of racism experienced by European populations is anti-Semitism. Jews organized themselves into communities, which lived among us, and despite segregation formed part of our world. There are no cases of racism involving populations or ethnic groups with which we do not have direct contact or which, although living among us, go unnoticed. This is the case, for example, for the Chinese who live, largely secluded, in Turin as in other major Italian cities, doing their job, which is usually as restaurateurs. In view of this, they are generally less noticeable in public than the *extra-comunitari*, whose survival depends on their trading around the streets. Besides the material fact of having to coexist on the same territory, which already in itself generates some friction, the presence of those considered different is the bearer of conflicts. This is due to the simple reason that a stranger enters our space primarily to survive by either lawful or unlawful means, and in so doing threatens our economic interests. This is demonstrated by the absence of the different forms of hideous racism towards tourist groups that visit our cities, or towards persons whose job does not threaten ours (Filipino maids are usually much appreciated), or towards distant populations with whom we have no contact. An example of this is that, as far as I am aware, Italians are not racist towards Eskimos. However, if suddenly hundreds of Eskimos were to invade our cities in search of work, the usual stereotypes would soon resurface: they are dirty, smelly, they have no intention of working, etc. As stated, racism emerges as an attitude of distrust for those who are different. But not everyone is different in the same way. There are different ways of being different.

If the material reason for the rising or outburst of a racist attitude is direct contact, where coexistence is not sought but, rather, forced, or there is a feared competition in the labour market, the mental tendency that allows racism to emerge is so-called ethnocentrism. Drawing on Tzvetan Todorov's admirable text, *On Human Diversity*, I define ethnocentrism as 'our' attitude towards 'others', or consisting of 'us' and 'them', which allows for the unwarranted establishment of the specific values of one's own society as universal values. This is asserted even when these values are derived from local and particularist customs. On the basis of these it is incorrect, if not foolish, and sometimes even absurd, to claim our superiority over those who belong to an ethnic group with different and similarly particularist customs. 'The ethnocentrist is thus a kind of caricature of the universalist.'[4] Every population tends to consider itself civilized and to reject other populations as barbarian. The contrast between us, the civilized, and others, the barbarian (usually the non-Europeans), spans the whole of Western history. Furthermore, this judgement is undermined by its mutual circularity, in that each population considers the other barbarian. In this regard, Italians are no better, and it would be unusual if they were. Eurocentrism, or the contrast between East and West, derived from the contrast between the Greeks, who considered themselves civilized because they were free, and the Persians, who were considered barbarians because they remained subjected without rebelling against their despots.[5] During the nineteenth century, the greater number of European philosophers was Eurocentric, as were also both Hegel and Marx. There is also a mitigated version of ethnocentrism, according to which, although our values do not claim to be universal and we are aware of this, we maintain moreover that there is no reason to renounce them. This less arrogant form of ethnocentrism generates the so-termed 'cultural relativism'. There are no superior or inferior populations. Each has its values and should retain them. Such an attitude does not provoke aversion but rather, if anything, separation.

The phenomenology and ideologies of racism

There are also various kinds of what is considered different in behaviours that from time to time are adopted towards 'others'. These are persons whom we consider different to ourselves, or are not the same as us, and thus extend them a differentiated treatment. But there are different levels of treatment, which depend on both the subjective qualities and objective circumstances. At the lowest level there is the simple verbal mockery, such as referring to southern Italians as 'terroni' [peasants], and to African immigrants as 'vu cumprà?' [will you buy?]. At the higher level there are: avoidance, the refusal to become involved with them in any way, keeping at a distance but without going as far as behaving in a hostile manner, exhibiting indifference, showing a certain discomfort in their presence, edging away when they approach, and so on. Moving up to a higher level there is the type of discrimination which can be regarded as the origin of institutional racism. This type of discrimination represents the non-recognition of rights, above all, the individual rights to which every person is entitled as a human being. These are rights of liberty and property rights, and progressively other major social rights, such as access to basic education.[6] Along with discrimination there is usually segregation, which consists of preventing those who are different from mixing with those who are the same. This is effected by locating them in a separate area, generally in degraded city zones, constraining them to live exclusively with their own kind, and thus preventing assimilation. In short, those who are different must remain so. The highest level is that of aggression against single individuals, which begins as a sporadic and random act, and ends in premeditated and mass extermination.

Reaching the highest from the lowest levels is achieved by moving through a real qualitative jump. But between these there is yet another attitude. This is no longer racism as a spontaneous and non-reflective attitude towards those who are different, who without being asked become part of one's community and threaten one's job or one's identity, but racism as ideology. Unlike the former, this is a conscious and documented doctrine that claims to be based on facts, capable of being scientifically proven, and can even be transformed into a complete albeit perverse vision of the world. The difference between racism as a natural reaction to the intrusive and threatening invasion by those who are different and racism as ideology is so vast that Todorov goes as far as proposing two different terms for them: *racisme* for the first, and *racialisme* for the other. Unfortunately, this distinction is not usually made in common language, from which derive false answers and inadequate remedies. When the question of whether Italians are racist is posed, we refer to the first meaning of the word. Conversely, if we ask whether racism exists in the tradition of Italian thought, we refer above all to the second meaning. It is one thing to ask what the behaviour of Italians is towards foreigners in general, and immigrants in particular. It is another to ask whether there are racist doctrines in the history of Italian thought, such as those that existed in France and Germany.

In order to be able to speak of racist ideology (or theory) the following three conditions are required, and can be defined as the premises for racism as a world vision.

(1) Humanity is divided into different races, whose diversity is given by biological and psychological elements, and ultimately also cultural, with the latter deriving from the former. The existence of races means that there are human groups with constant characteristics, which are inherently transmitted. This is not the place to discuss the scientific basis of this doctrine, whose veracity has had many supporters in the

past, because it is only one of the premises of racist ideology. It is scientifically unfounded and relatively harmless, since what derives from this in practice is a policy of separation and condemnation of mixed races.

(2) The assertion that there are not only different races but also superior and inferior races allows racist ideology to move forward. However, it confronts the difficulty of providing the criteria on the basis of which it can be established with certainty that one race is superior to another. The criteria adopted from time to time can be the aesthetic: 'We are beautiful and they are ugly'; intellectual: 'We are intelligent and they are stupid'; or moral: 'We are good and they are evil.' Often racist ideologies contain a mix of these three criteria. Even this second premise does not have con- sequences that are inherently negative. It is possible to argue that, once a relation between superior and inferior is verified, the former since it is superior has the duty to protect the inferior, to train, educate, and help them achieve the highest levels of those values which the superior maintains itself to be the bearer. This depicts the type of relation that exists between parents and their minor-age children. In the history of political institutions, there is a form of government defined as paternalism. It recognizes the sovereign as superior to his subjects, who are likened to minor-age children, and as such the sovereign must behave towards them like an affec- tionate and benevolent father.

(3) It is further stated that not only are there races, as well as superior and inferior races, but the superior, precisely because they are that, have the right to dominate the inferior races, and probably derive from them all possible advantages. The justification of colonialism used primarily the second principle. Not too long ago, the Soviet Union justified its aggression of Afghanistan by maintaining that it had the duty to provide fraternal support to its neighbour, which was threatened by powerful enemies. Nevertheless, racism never renounced the use of the above-mentioned third prin- ciple. One does not need to read Hitler's *Mein Kampf* to find

phrases where it is peremptorily asserted that the superior races must dominate the inferior. Already at the time of triumphant colonialism there were those who stated, as did the historian and philosopher Ernest Renan, that 'the conquest of a country of inferior race by a superior race that settles there to govern it is not at all shocking'.[7] It is only with Hitler's coming to power, however, that for the first time in the history of civilized Europe 'a racial state' was formed.[8] It was a racial state in the fullest meaning of the term, because it pursued race purity. This was effected by eliminating not only individuals of other races, but also those of its own who were either physically or psychologically inferior, such as the terminally ill, the mentally disabled, and the elderly who were no longer self-sufficient.

The distinction between a racist behaviour and the ideology of racism has for years been present, because in Italy we are confronted above all with the first. An actual Italian racist ideology does not exist. Even during fascism's anti-Semitic campaign there were few, or barely noticeable, attempts to accommodate racist ideologies that had succeeded elsewhere. To date, in Italy what exists is the 'background noise' I mentioned above. If there is a problem concerning racism here, it exists above all with regard to spontaneous racism. Nor are there any racist parties, such as those that already exist in France (le Pen) and Germany (the Republikaner).[9] While it is true that there is no need for a racist party in order for racism to emerge, it is undeniable that the formation of such a party would strengthen it. Likewise, there is no need for a racist ideology for racial conflicts to develop. With the advent of mass immigration where populations with different customs, language, traditions, and religion come into direct contact, racial conflict is inevitable. Prejudice, which as stated earlier can take root in every individual, is sufficient to spark a conflict. However, combating prejudice is not sufficient to resolve the ethnic conflicts now emerging in many parts of the globe, especially in those countries with high immigration, Italy included.

For a universalist education

Since the emergence of ethnic conflicts cannot be altogether avoided, in order at least to contain it, an immigration policy is needed. I will not dwell on this aspect, as it is outside both my intended scope and my specific competence. I limit my comments to saying that immigration policies are located at two extremes. At one end, there is assimilation, which leads to the progressive homologation of immigrants with the original inhabitants of the host country. This occurs through the gradual recognition of citizenship rights, the principal of which is a political right. Citizenship rights, however, must be distinguished from individual rights, which every state under the rule of law must guarantee to everyone. At the other end, instead, there is a respect for differences that allows immigrants to preserve, in the broadest possible sense, whatever makes them different, such as their language, cultural rites, and customs. Between the two extremes there are solutions by compromise, which depend on several factors that vary from country to country. The choice between the two extremes also depends on the greater or lesser entrenchment of mutual prejudices held by the two conflicting parties.

There is no other way to combat racial prejudice than through education oriented towards universal values.[10] There are many forms of universalism which, despite differences of race, traditions, and generation (the generational difference is added to all the others and is not at all negligible), share a common humanity that traverses all differences of time and place. Beginning from Christianity, universalism proceeds through the doctrine of natural law to reach Kantian morals, or a rationalized Christianity, which according to its fundamental maxim means 'to respect the human being as a person'. I would not exclude from these universalistic morals the English empiricists' ethics of 'moral sentiments'. Universalist and ethical conceptions are those that have as the ultimate aim of history the establishment of an, albeit ideal, *civitas maxima*, or the city for all. From this perspective, all individuals are regarded as citizens of the world, and thus over and above all other homelands. This is the ideal that inspired the foundation of the United Nations in the wake of the massacre of World War II. One of the highest expressions of such universalism is the Universal Declaration of the Rights of Man, through which every individual is potentially a subject of international law.

Universalist education and democracy, moreover, proceed at the same pace, whereas democracy and racism are incompatible, for at least two reasons. First, unlike autocratic governments, democracy is inspired by universal principles such as liberty, justice, respect for others, tolerance, and nonviolence. Instead, racism is antiliberal, anti-egalitarian, intolerant, and, in extreme cases, violent and criminal (as Auschwitz showed). Second, democracy is inclusive because its aim is to allow 'outsiders' into its domain, and extend its benefits to them also; the first of which is respect for all faiths. During the nineteenth century and up to the present, democratization has been a process of gradual inclusion of individuals who were previously excluded. The fact that not all individuals can be included, in the same way as not everything and everyone can be tolerated, is a practical problem for which appropriate solutions must be found for different circumstances. Democracy, however, cannot be 'exclusive' without negating its intrinsic essence of an 'open society'.

There is no need to contrive philosophical arguments for one to be convinced of the essential unity of humanity. It is sufficient to look at a child's face anywhere in the world. When we observe a child, who represents the human being closest to nature, and who has not yet been moulded or corrupted by the customs of a particular country, the only detectable differences between a Chinese, African, Indian, or Italian child are the somatic traits. When we witness a Somali mother crying over her child, who is either dead or emaciated, is she any different to other mothers? Are not her tears the same as those shed by any mother in the world? There is no more convincing evidence of this fundamental and original equality than the growing trend of adoptions of children who belong to societies completely different to ours, and with which attitudes of racial aversion between adults could emerge in certain circumstances.

Nevertheless universalistic education is not sufficient if it cannot be translated into corresponding action. Neither education nor political institutions are sufficient. What becomes increasingly more necessary is action from below. Here, the highly topical subject of the contribution of voluntary organizations is considered pertinent, and in the wake of the crisis, or rather the degeneration, of the welfare state it has also attracted some attention. To date, institutions have not fulfilled their task. Hence the only other remedy for such state insufficiency is the emergence of initiatives by civil society. We are almost witnessing an actual historical recurrence, since the welfare state emerged to render unnecessary charitable works. Today, because the welfare state has been unable to meet society's contingent needs, charitable works reveal their persisting vitality.

In any case, the work of voluntary organizations and institutions should proceed at the same pace, because they are both necessary and complement each other. Each operates within its ambit. Voluntary work is directed at supporting single individuals. Institutions, for their part, are concerned with the elaboration of immigration policies that aim to avoid, or at least reduce, the severity of ethnic conflict.[11]

Notes

1. The volume was published in 1992 by Rosenberg and Sellier, Turin. The citations are found on p. 27. See also L. Balbo and L. Manconi, *Razzismi: Un vocabolario* [*Racisms: A Vocabulary*] (Milan, Feltrinelli 1993); R. Bastide, *Noi e gli altri: I luoghi di incontro e di separazione culturali e razziali* [*Us and Others: Places for Cultural and Racial Encounter and Separation*], tr. Bruno Maffeis (Milan, Jaca Books 1986); T. Ben Jelloun, *Il razzismo spiegato a mia figlia* [*Racism Explained to My Daughter*] (Milan, Bompiani 1997); R. Gallissot and A. Rivera, *L'imbroglio etnico: In dieci parole chiave* [*The Ethnic Conundrum: Ten Key Words*], intro. M. Kilami (Bari, Dedalo 1997); M. Wieviorka, *Lo spazio del razzismo* [*The Space of Racism*], intro.

Laura Balbo (Milan, EST 1996); G. Zincone, *Uno schermo contro il razzismo: Per una politica dei diritti utili* [*A Defence Against Racism: A Policy for Due Rights*], with a study by A. Lostia and G. Tomaino (Rome, Donzelli 1994).

2. P. A. Taguieff, *La force du préjugé: Essai sur le racisme et ses doubles* (Paris, Editions de la découverte 1987), tr. M. Canosa and P. Cristalli (eds) as *La forza del pregiudizio: Saggio sul razzismo e l'antirazzismo* [*The Force of Prejudice: An Essay on Racism and Antiracism*] (Bologna, Il Mulino 1994).

3. I draw this and other citations from Taguieff, ibid. Montesquieu's passage is cited on p. 274.

4. T. Todorov, *On Human Diversity: Nationalism, Racism and Exoticism in French Thought* (Cambridge MA, Harvard University Press 1993), p. 1.

5. On the subject of foreigners, in general, see the collection of essays *Lo straniero, ovvero l'identità culturale a confronto* [*Strangers, or Cultural Identity Compared*] (Bari, Laterza 1991), and in particular the essay by M. Moggi, 'Straniero due volte: il barbaro e il mondo greco' ['Twice a stranger: the barbarian and the Greek world'], pp. 51–76. Among others, the author cites Euripides, who considered the domination of the Greeks over the barbarians legitimate, rather than vice versa.

6. On the fundamental distinction between individual rights and citizenship rights, which is well understood by jurists but not usually as clear to sociologists, see the essay by L. Ferrajoli, 'Cittadinanza e diritti fondamentali' ['Citizenship and fundamental rights'], *Teoria politica* (1993), 3, pp. 63–76; a more extensive discussion, 'Dai diritti del cittadino ai diritti della persona' ['From citizenship rights to individual rights'], is included in D. Zolo (ed.), *La cittadinanza: Appartenenza, identità, diritti* [*Citizenship: Belonging, Identity, Rights*] (Rome/Bari, Laterza 1994), with a postscript by S. Rodota, pp. 263–92.

7. Cited in Todorov, *On Human Diversity*, p. 112, originally in E. Renan, *La réforme intellectuelle et morale en France* [*Intellectual and Moral Reformation in France*], 1, p. 390.

8. This is the title of M. Burleigh and W. Wippermann, *The Racial State: Germany, 1933–1945* (New York, Cambridge University Press 1991).

9. See L. Balbo and L. Manconi, *I razzismi reali* [*Existing Racisms*] (Milan, Feltrinelli 1992), p. 89. By the same authors, the acknowledged promoters of Associazione Italia-Razzismo, see also *I razzismi possibili* [*Possible Racisms*] (Milan, Feltrinelli 1990).

10. See L. Operti and L. Cometti (eds), *Verso un'educazione interculturale* [*Towards an Intercultural Education*], promoted by IRRSAE Piemonte (Turin, Bollati Boringhieri 1992), a collection of both general and specific writings on 'other cultures' and on the conditions of immigrants in Turin. See also F. Crespi and R. Segatori, *Multiculturalismo e democrazia* [*Multiculturalism and Democracy*] (Rome, Donzelli 1996), and A. Agosti (ed.), *Intercultura e insegnamento: Aspetti teorici e metodologici* [*Interculture and Education: Theoretical and Methodological Aspects*] (Turin, Società Editrice Internazionale 1996).

11. On the growing interest for voluntary institutions, I mention some recent books: *Volontari, volontariato Immagini* [*Volunteers, Voluntary institutions: Images*], texts by N. Bobbio and C. De Giacomi (Città di Castello, Petruzzi 1994); S. Gawronski, *Guida al volontariato: Un libro per chi vuol cominciare* [*A Guide to Voluntary Work: A Beginners' Book*], intro. Gianfranco Bettin (Turin, Einaudi 1997); B. Tomai, *Il volontariato: Istruzioni per l'uso* [*Voluntary Institutions and Their Use*], with contributions by C. Ranci, M. Campedelli, D. Bidussa, and G. Pescarolo (Milan, Feltrinelli 1994).

Part III

Truth and Liberty

That one cannot be tolerant without being sceptical is an old, worn-out, though comfortable argument supported by those who are intolerant. Gamaliel, the Hebrew doctor of law, advised his citizens against persecuting the Apostles (Acts V: 33–9). While in the religious controversies of the sixteenth century he was elevated as a hero of tolerance, Calvin instead called him 'a sceptic and a blind man groping in the dark'.[1] The aim of my address is to refute the argument by presenting some reasons (not at all exhaustive) which explain why one can be tolerant without being a sceptic. Here we are concerned with tolerance between philosophers. However, those who know the history of religious freedom will be aware that when the idea of tolerance emerged during the sixteenth and seventeenth centuries, it was not a product of religious indifference. Rather, if anything, it was the result of a faith that was not imposed but freely professed. It is not until we arrive, perhaps, beyond Pierre Bayle,[2] at the Enlightenment thinkers that we see the coupling of tolerance and scepticism.

To begin, I would like to free myself of a preliminary objection. This is that, contrary to what occurs in relations between religious faiths, which address the large masses rather than the initiated few, in relations between philosophies there would be a place for everyone. Therefore, the problem of tolerance, which is one of coexistence, would not arise. If this objection were well founded, our discussion would be completely useless. But I do not believe the objection is well founded. First, it is not true that in relations between philosophers there is always a place for everyone. To provide an almost true-to-life example, the contentions between philosophers concern limited resources, such as university chairs and academic positions. Here the problem of intolerance is alive and well. In the second place, in my view there is a tacit assumption in this whole discussion, in that when we say 'philosophy', we really mean 'ideology'. By this we understand a global conception of life that underpins, or is supposed to, any significant contemporary political or social movement. As a result, the difference from religious tolerance noted above does not hold. Sometimes when referring to Marxism we think of socialist movements; with spiritualism we think of Christian-inspired parties; and with empiricism or pragmatism we think of movements that promote lay and radical democracy. However, those who claim there is a place for everyone take for granted, and without debate, the solution of one of the most serious problems of our time.

I separate the arguments in favour of tolerance, according to whether they are based on a monistic or pluralistic conception of truth. Within each of the two series, I consider four arguments.

(1) The first argument that comes to mind is as far away from scepticism as one can imagine. It can be formulated as follows: 'I am tolerant of the faiths of others because I believe in the expansive strength of truth.' For those who support this argument there is only one truth, theirs, or that held by others who think like them. The faiths of others are errors. However, the clouds of error that obfuscate their minds will lift and disappear, and the sunshine of truth will eventually prevail. What is the aim, therefore, of preventing error by persecution? Is not persecution of the error perhaps an unnecessary and dangerous correction of a predetermined historic design? This claim is promoted by an optimistic conception of history, where history is conceived as governed by divine Providence, or by an immanent Spirit. Although common in the history of religious tolerance, mainly through the work of the solitary heretics who drew their strength from trust in God's kingdom, in the history of philosophical liberty this

argument reminds us of the romantic conception of history. In Italy, this was so well personified by Croce and his theory of history as the history of liberty. According to this conception, freedom is bound to prevail because it is a winner even when it succumbs. In contrast, a pessimist like Gaetano Mosca stated persistently that a theory that prescribed liberty as a remedy would be ridiculed by future generations, because it was simplistic and impractical. I recall an anecdote about De Sanctis as recounted by Croce. It depicts De Sanctis as a prisoner, chanting the refrain: 'He always wins, always wins, and even when he loses, he still wins', to which the guard asks: 'Who wins?' The prisoner replies: 'Silly man! Don't you understand that what always wins, even when losing, is Liberty.'[3]

(2) One can believe that there is only one truth, but despite this conviction it is not likely that it can overcome error other than through an arduous and risky process. At this point, there is a need to understand if the method that will enable one's truth to prevail is the recourse to persuasion or to force. In other words, whether one proceeds to disprove the error, or to persecute the errant. The person who chooses the first path is tolerant. Nevertheless, would anyone be prepared to say that this person's renunciation of the truth espoused is greater than that of the person who follows the second path? What was surrendered was simply a certain approach that allowed the truth to prevail. Leaving aside any moral judgement, it is a surrender that, together with a better-disposed attitude towards the interlocutor's intelligence, reveals a greater trust in one's ideas than does the opposite. Substituting the method of force with that of persuasion was a recurrent topic in the history of the Reformation. In Thomas More's *Utopia*, it appears in exemplary form:

> Utopus was certain that to try to compel everyone else by means of threats and violence to believe what you yourself happen to believe is both arrogant and ineffectual. Should it be the case that there is only one true religion, and all the rest are false, he was quite confident that, as long as people con-

fined themselves to moderate and reasonable discussion, the truth would have the advantage and would eventually prevail.[4]

Since in philosophy we are all in complete agreement about tolerance, understood as renouncing the use of secular force to make one's ideas prevail, it is pointless to insist. However, should we need a citation, Locke provides one:

> For the truth certainly would do well enough if she were once left to shift for herself. She seldom has received and, I fear, never will receive much assistance from the power of great men, to whom she is but rarely known and more rarely welcome. She is not taught by laws, nor has she any need of force to procure her entrance into the minds of men. Errors indeed prevail by the assistance of foreign and borrowed succours. But if truth makes not her way into the understanding by her own light, she will be but the weaker for any borrowed force violence can add to her.[5]

I doubt that philosophers, even in recent times, have in fact always been faithful to this rule, given that at a philosophy congress Piero Martinetti, a philosopher dear to me, pronounced the following memorable words: 'I could not... as a philosopher and citizen of the world in which there are no persecutions or excommunications, become the executor of an excommunication decree.'[6]

(3) There is only one truth and it is my truth. This is not likely to overcome error, either through the providential law of history (the first thesis), or through the greater intensity of its persuasive force (second thesis): error is bound to survive alongside truth. I accept it for the sake of a moral principle, which is respect for the other person. Seemingly, it is a case of conflict between theoretical reason and practical reason, and between the logic of reason and the logic of the heart. In effect, it is a conflict between two moral principles: the morals of coherence that lead me to place my truth above everything else, and the morals of benevolence, of respect. The principle of freedom of conscience that in the end pre-

vailed over the wars of religion emerged from this, not from indifference, but from a deep understanding that in every person there is something inaccessible and unviolable, which used to be referred to as the inner sanctuary of conscience. In Jean Bodin's *Heptaplomeres*, the seven wise men who participate in the discussion, after each presents his idea in homage to freedom of conscience, decide from then on to refrain from any debate on religious matters, though each retains his religious freedom. Today, with the diffusion of personalistic conceptions of philosophy, this point of view should have become familiar. I read in Mounier: 'To cease placing myself from my point of view and place myself from that of the other. Not just to find myself in another chosen the same as me; not just to know the other as a generalized knowledge; but to embrace his singularity from the depth of my singularity, in an act of acceptance and an effort of reconnection.'[7] There is therefore an aspect of moral personalism that fits the attitude of tolerance, and can be expressed in this maxim: 'Act according to conscience and operate in such a way that others are not persuaded to act against their conscience.' A maxim of this kind aims to preserve truth without making it an instrument of condemnation or death for the error of others.

(4) Since tolerance is a practical attitude, along with moral reasons there can be those of a utilitarian nature: tolerance as the lesser evil. They are reasons that change in proportion to the relations of force between me, or my sect or school, as holders of the truth, and the others who are steeped in error. If I am the stronger, accepting error can be a judicious act. Persecution can cause a scandal, which reveals the flaw I would like to conceal. An error is propagated more through persecution than through silence. On the other hand, if I am the weaker, enduring error is a prudent act. Were I to rebel, I would be crushed and the small seed would be lost. Even here, one hopes that silence would be more fruitful than an act of desperation or rebellion. If we are on a par, then the principle of reciprocity comes into play, and tolerance becomes an act of interpersonal justice. When I claim the

right to persecute others, I unwittingly give others the right to persecute me. Today it is you, tomorrow it will be me. In all three cases, tolerance is a calculation that has nothing to do with my way of understanding truth.

The attitudes considered up to this point are more frequent in religious or ideological controversy than in the philosophical proper. Exclusive faith that leads to a clear separation between truth and error is intrinsic to a religious person. A philosopher is open to doubt, and persists with the search. Once the destination is reached, it is but a stage in an endless voyage, and one needs to be always ready to set sail. However, there is a difference between the search of the man of faith and that of the man of reason. While the first searches for what he has already found, the other, sometimes, does not even find what he has most intensely sought. Nevertheless, what is not exclusivism is not necessarily scepticism. If by exclusivism we mean the attitude for which one theory is true, and by scepticism we mean the attitude for which no theory is true, between the two there is a place for the attitude that allows for many theories to exist. So far we have considered certain aspects of an exclusive conception of truth. In the following discussion we shall consider some aspects of the conception which by contrast we can term inclusive, because instead of one truth there are many. In the former aspects, as we have seen, tolerance can be an expedient, or a lesser evil. In the latter, it is something much more important. It is a necessary condition for the life and development of philosophical thought. In that life, the philosophy of freedom and the freedom of philosophy, rather than opposing each other, are completely integrated.

(1) Let us first consider the fairly frequent attitude by which it is believed that to formulate a total conception of reality, there is a need to manipulate several theories, even apparently opposed, to reconcile, fuse, or merge them into one. Adopting a term also derived from religious controversies, we can call this 'syncretism'. If an exclusivist person can be tolerant through calculation, a syncretist is tolerant by neces-

sity. In the face of important philosophical or ideological controversies, syncretism cannot be appeased other than by the conviction of their obvious uselessness. However, to render this demonstration possible, each theory must be expressed, exposed, combined, and compared with opposite theories. During the Reformation, as is well known, syncretism was one of the ideals of Christian humanism and Erasmian irenism. If we survey contemporary philosophy, fields that are more or less lasting and authoritative, and which I tend to regard as deriving from the syncretist combination, are as follows: the reconciliation of idealism with spiritualism, of idealism with existentialism, of existentialism with spiritualism; then the reconciliation of Marxism with pragmatism, of neopositivism with historicism, and lastly, of Marxism with neopositivism. During the period of the most passionate search for a point of convergence in a divided world, we witnessed the most reckless of syncretist operations. This was the reconciliation of communism with Christianity, sometimes, in more strictly philosophical terms, virtually of Marxism and Thomism. A syncretist can be accused of making impure mixes, but he is not a sceptic. Moreover, if there is a reproach that can be advanced it is that of believing too much rather than too little in the truth of others.

(2) Eclectism is different to syncretism. For an eclectic person, every system contains a mix of truth and error. Therefore, no system has the privilege of being the only true one, and similarly, no system can be entirely false. The person who more than anyone may hold the truth is someone who does not reject anything of the theories advanced by different schools, but can wisely accept and retain the grain of truth contained in each. While a syncretist aims at mixing two or more systems, an eclectic aims to form a new system by arranging the fragments of truth wherever they can be found. As is well known, the development of eclectism is closely connected with the history of liberalism. Based on his theory of the happy medium between rationalism and empiricism, and between the monarchy and the bourgeoisie,

Victor Cousin declared himself,[8] at the same time and for the same reason, to be a philosopher of eclectism and a theorist of moderate liberalism during the Restoration. However, the tolerance practised by an eclectic does not derive, once again, from indifference, as with the sceptic, but from the belief that there is some truth in every theory. Moreover, truth is the product of a compromise, or of a reconciliation of different theories. In the ideological controversy we witness daily I tend to regard as eclectic, even if with some hesitation, the various positions known as the 'third way', and as syncretist those of pro-Marxist Christianity. Syncretism and eclecticism, which emerged during the time of the wars of religion and in the wake of the Napoleonic wars respectively, express an irenic exigency. It is not accidental that the upheaval caused by World War II produced some quite obvious embodiments of both of them.

(3) A third and widely diffused position, above all in contemporary philosophy, can be formulated as follows: 'There are necessarily many theories, all true, but each is true at its time and in its place.' This is the thesis of historicism, which is different from both syncretism and eclecticism. These share the conviction that the whole truth is always the result, or the combination, of many partial truths. For historicism, any truth is, in that particular historical situation, the only truth, but since historical conditions change, truth changes with them: *veritas filia temporis* [truth is the daughter of time]. There is a need, however, to distinguish between the two versions of historicism: the absolutist and the relativist. Absolute historicism, which combines the claim of the historicity of truth with that of the rationality of history, according to which every stage includes both the preceding and the following, should strictly speaking lead more to intolerance. Those who are convinced they embody a necessary phase of the development of the absolute Spirit will claim the right to overwhelm those who hinder their progress. Often the idealization of history, however, is corrected by a dialectical conception of truth. According to this, every historically given theory is partial, and truth emerges from contrast and the

synthesis of opposites. The theory of tolerance instead is relativist historicism, according to which the assertion of the historicity of truth does not imply a providential conception of history. The different theories coexist on different levels in the various social contexts, in a relation of mutual integration rather than of exclusion. From the perspective of the philosophy of history, relativist historicism replaces that of the sociology of knowledge. The popular version of relativist historicism is perspectivism. An example of the close nexus between perspectivism and democratic theory is found in Hans Kelsen, one of the best-known theorists of liberal democracy in contemporary thought.[9]

(4) The most radical attempt to realize the endless multiplication of truths, and contemporaneously reject the sceptical solution, is personalism. According to this philosophy, every truth is personal. Its hallmark consists of the fact that it always reveals a being that is at the same time total and singular. Of the two versions of personalism, the spiritualist places the emphasis more on the totality, the existentialist more on the singularity, but in respect of our problem, which is that of tolerance, they lead to the same consequences. That truth is personal in the end means that the multiplicity of truths is justified by the multiplicity and irreducibility of individuals. Every truth comes into the world through a being that leaves its mark, and each of these beings is irreducible to another. Since this being is the only instrument of truth, it follows that truths are many, infinite, and all validly proposed. In other words, they all deserve to be heard. Ontological personalism, to which we refer here, is not to be confused with the more common form of ethical personalism, which has already been mentioned. Moreover, there are different arguments that each advances in support of tolerance. According to ethical personalism, tolerance is a moral duty, and is owed out of respect for the person, irrespective of the truth possessed. With ontological personalism, tolerance is owed out of respect for truth, which when it is revealed by the person transcends it, and is receptive to the truth of others. In the theory of truth, consider the importance that

the will to communicate has for Karl Jaspers.[10] The conception of truth as revelation of the individual can lead to the mystic solution of incommunicability or to the personalistic inherent to communication. The irreducible multiplicity of truths is corrected, for example, by the will to communicate, and only at the point where communication fails does silence begin.

I have sought to demonstrate that there are many reasons why one can be tolerant without being sceptical. I do not think that it would be difficult to demonstrate the obverse of the coin: that is, the reasons why sometimes one can be both sceptical and intolerant. Those who do not believe in truth will be tempted to submit every decision and every choice to force. This would be based on the principle that since one cannot command what is just, the just is what is commanded. In a chapter of his *La filosofia dell'autorità*, aptly titled 'Scepticism and authority', Giuseppe Rensi wrote the following as a kind of epigraph to his discussion: 'Scepticism generates a philosophy of authority: a philosophy of authority can only be based on scepticism.'[11]

Notes

1. I draw the citation from J. Leclerc, *Histoire de la tolérance au siècle de la Réforme* [*History of Tolerance in the Age of Reformation*] (Paris, Aubier 1955), I, p. 337.
2. [Translator's note: Pierre Bayle (1647–1706) was a noted French sceptical philosopher and critic, and an influential leader of the modern sceptical movement. In 1693 he was removed from his professorship at the Protestant academy of Rotterdam on account of his sceptical opinions.]
3. B. Croce, *Cultura e vita morale*, 2nd edn (Bari, Laterza 1926), p. 288.
4. T. Moro, *Utopia*, ed. and tr. David Wootton (Indianapolis, Hackett 1999), p. 147.
5. J. Locke, *A Letter Concerning Toleration* (The Hague, Martinus Nijhoff 1963), p. 79.

6. P. Martinetti, 'I congressi filosofici e la funzione religiosa e sociale della filosofia', *Rivista di filosofia* (1944), XXXV, p. 102.

7. E. Mounier, *Personalism* (Notre Dame, University of Notre Dame Press 1970), p. 21.

8. [Translator's note: Victor Cousin (1792–1867) was a French philosopher and statesman. He was first a follower of the Scottish psychological school, but later under German influence developed a kind of eclecticism.]

9. [Translator's note: Hans Kelsen (1891–1973), the Austrian jurist and legal philosopher, is known for the most rigorous development of a 'positivist' theory of law, that is, one that excludes from its analysis any ethical, political, or historical considerations, and finds the essence of the legal order in the 'black letter' or laid-down (posited) law. Kelsen held a monistic view of the world, and expresses his philosophical relativism through his perspective that democratic tolerance presupposes a relativistic view. In developing his concept of 'peace through law' in the 1940s, Kelsen's perspectivism made a major contribution to international criminal law, as relevant now as it was then.]

10. [Translator's note: Karl Jaspers (1883–1969), a German philosopher, was one of the founders of existentialism. He contended that philosophical truth is a function of communication with the other and with myself, and 'is the truth I live by and do not merely think about'.]

11. G. Rensi, *La filosofia dell'autorità* [*The Philosophy of Authority*] (Palermo, Sandron 1920), pp. 234–5.

Tolerance and Truth

The idea of tolerance emerges and develops within the domain of religious controversies. The great defenders of tolerance, from Locke to Voltaire, fought all forms of intolerance, which for centuries stained Europe with blood. This occurred following the breakdown of religious universalism, which resulted from the practices of the reformed churches and heretical sects. Gradually, the principle of tolerance shifted from the domain of religious controversies to the sphere of political debates, or to the clash between ideologies that are the modern form of religion. Recognition of religious freedom led to non-confessional, or secular, states, in the same way as recognition of political freedom allowed democratic states to emerge. Both types of state are the highest expression of the lay spirit that characterized the beginning of modern Europe. Such lay, or secular, spirit is understood as a way of thinking that entrusts the fate of the *regnum hominis* [human realm] to critical reason rather than to religious inspiration. Although such a spirit does not fail to recognize the value of sincere personal faith, it leaves its profession to individual free will.

Although widely recognized as a rule of coexistence, and therefore as a practical rule, the principle of tolerance needs to be defended continually. On the theoretical level, this is effected against the accusation of being the expression of religious indifference, or even of irreligious mentality. In his *Instruction pastorale* Jacques Bossuet designates and criticizes tolerance as indifference towards religion (which is only one, and this only is true).[1] In the overall tradition of church teaching, the term 'tolerance' is understood in a limited sense as 'enduring' an error, for the simple reason of practical expedience. While respect is directed towards something considered right, tolerance is exercised towards something considered wrong, which although preventable is not prevented for reasons of prudence.

However, this restrictive, or even negative, meaning of tolerance does not belong only to the tradition of religious thought. A case in point is the debate that emerged in Italy at the beginning of the century between two Italian authors, who were both supporters of lay culture. Luigi Luzzatti in 1909 wrote *La libertà di coscienza e di scienza* [*Liberty of Conscience and Science*], where he praised tolerance because he quite rightly considered it the inspiring principle of the liberal state. This principle enabled both the philosophical affirmation and legal recognition of the rights of liberty, *in primis* the freedoms of religion and of opinion. Benedetto Croce, the major philosopher of the time, replied to Luzzatti, taking up the defence of intolerance, maintaining that tolerance is a practical principle, and arguing that of itself, it is not an absolute good. It has a relative value, but is not always valuable. He further stated, in terms so strong as to be considered outrageous by many people, that 'the noblest and most heroic individuals were not always to be found' among those who professed tolerance. 'Often these were the rhetoricians and the indifferent, while the strong-hearted slaughtered and were being slaughtered.' He concluded sharply: 'A lovely word, tolerance! In life, no one is tolerant because everyone has something to defend, and if we no longer erect the stake it is because our customs no longer allow it.'[2]

It is interesting to observe how Croce, the lay philosopher, attributes the same negative meaning to tolerance as that attributed by traditional Catholic teaching. In other words, in both cases the negative meaning of the word derives from its being interpreted as the expression of one's indifference in the face of truth. This is the attitude of someone who does not believe in any truth, and for whom all truths are equally debatable. It follows that for a religious person tolerance can be practised only as a lesser evil, and only when it is absolutely necessary to uphold one's avowed truth. When Croce states that tolerance is a 'practical and contingent formula' he uses, perhaps unconsciously, the language of theologians.

For tolerance to acquire a positive meaning, there was a need for it to be considered no longer a mere rule of caution, or the endurance of evil, or of an error, for reasons of practical expediency. It was also necessary for the freedoms of religion and thought, guaranteed by the proper application of the rule of tolerance, to be recognized as the best condition that would allow one's truth to prevail through persuasion rather than by imposition. This does not mean, however, that everyone shares this optimistic conviction of the expanding strength of truth. Nevertheless, despite the fact that it is not universally shared, this conviction, upheld fervently, for example, by Thomas More in his depiction of the imaginary island, opens the way for a new, even deeper, and ethically more authoritative reason to support the principle of tolerance, which is respect for the conscience of others. This reason is based on the principle universally recognized by civilized nations in national and international declarations of rights: the right to freedom of conscience.

The distinction between tolerance in the negative sense, simply as endurance of an error, and tolerance in the positive sense enables us to understand how one can also speak about intolerance in the positive and negative sense. Tolerance is not always a virtue, or intolerance a vice. I recalled earlier what Croce observed about those individuals who profess to be tolerant, often out of weakness rather than meekness. There are two ways of considering this issue. In the same way in which intolerance, contrary to positive tolerance, is always negative when understood as a constraint on consciences in practice, or as a dogmatic assertion of an absolute truth that disallows objections in theory, so is intolerance not always negative when it opposes negative tolerance. This is the tolerance of a sceptic, which is the replicate antithesis of a dogmatic's intolerance, or the tolerance of a morally indifferent person, which is the replicate antithesis of a fanatic's intolerance. Although in practice it is difficult to differentiate them, the distinction must be kept in mind.

The question is generally asked in the following terms: are there limits to tolerance? If so, where should the boundaries be set? There are no completely intolerant societies, neither do absolutely tolerant societies exist, except in Big Brother's absolute state, or in a similarly imaginary society that upholds the following maxim, 'If there is no God, everything is allowed.' However, between these two simply imaginary extremes, there are many intermediate levels.

During the years of the student movement, Herbert Marcuse's essay 'Repressive tolerance' enjoyed a certain success. He condemned the limited tolerance that was being practised in the United States where only ideas that, in his view, were conservative, or even reactionary, were tolerated. In contrast, progressive ideas aimed at a radical transformation of society were thwarted. Marcuse maintained that there should be a '[w]ithdrawal of tolerance from regressive movements *before* they can become active'. That is, before their success led to the loss of freedom by all.[3] In my view, the way in which Marcuse posed the problem is unsatisfactory, because it is based on the criterion of distinction between progressive and reactionary ideas, which lends itself to subjective evaluation. The core of the idea of tolerance is the recognition of equal rights for opposing theories, and therefore of the right to err, at least when the error is made in good faith. The need for tolerance emerges when one becomes conscious of the irreducibility of opinions, and of the necessity to find a *modus vivendi* between them. Between tolerance and persecution *tertium non datur* [a third way is not given]. If the tolerance Marcuse criticizes and terms repressive is persecutory, one cannot understand why the tolerance that he does approve is not persecutory for the same reasons, at least for those persons whom he excludes. Therefore, to exclude certain ideas from tolerance based on the distinction between progressive and reactionary ideas is dangerous, to say the least.

The only criterion on the basis of which a limitation of the rule of tolerance can be considered legitimate is that implicit in the idea of tolerance itself. Briefly, this can be formulated as follows: all ideas must be tolerated except those which deny the very idea of tolerance. The question is usually framed in these terms: should one tolerate those who are intolerant?

Of course, even this criterion of distinction, which in theory seems perfectly clear, in practice is not quite so easy to implement as it appears. The reason for that lies in the fact that there are different gradations of intolerance, as well as different spheres where intolerance can become evident. Such a criterion cannot be accepted unreservedly for a significant reason. Those who believe in the validity of tolerance do so because they are aware of the irreducibility of faiths and opinions, and of the consequent necessity not to impoverish the variety of expressions of human thought by prohibitions, but also because they believe that it is fruitful. They further maintain that the only way to induce the intolerant to accept tolerance is not persecution, but the recognition of their right to free expression. While it may be legally correct to respond to an intolerant person with intolerance, such a response is certainly ethically reprehensible and perhaps also politically impractical. This is not to say that once the intolerant are accepted into the sphere of liberty they will comprehend the ethical value of respect for the ideas of others. But it is certain that an intolerant person who is persecuted and excluded is unlikely to become enlightened. It may be worth risking liberty by allowing its enemy also to benefit, if the only alternative is restricting it until it is stifled, or prevented from achieving all its aims. It is better to have expansive liberty always threatened than a protected liberty which as such is incapable of evolving. Only threatened liberty is capable of renewal. Conversely, liberty that is incapable of renewal will become eventually a new kind of bondage.

The choice between the two attitudes is an ultimate one, and, as with all ultimate choices, it is of the kind that cannot be maintained solely with rational arguments. There are then historical conditions that now favour one, now the other. We must be prepared to acknowledge that the choice of one or the other allows us to distinguish a restrictive conception of tolerance, which is inherent to a conservative liberalism, from the extensive conception, which is intrinsic to a radical or progressive liberalism.

Here are two illuminating examples. The conservative Gaetano Mosca rejected as naive and foolish the theory according to which violence is powerless against truth and liberty. He observed that unfortunately history had shown itself to be more on the side of the intolerant than the tolerant, and had proven wrong those who maintained that truth would always prevail over persecution. He commented that future generations would deride this theory of the radical liberals.[4] On the other hand, at the time when Italy was beginning the restoration of our freedoms following the collapse of fascism, Luigi Einaudi stated: 'Those who believe in the idea of liberty ... argue that a party has the right to participate fully in political life even when it is openly opposed to freedom. Free individuals must not, in order to survive, deny their reason for living, the very liberty they profess to uphold.'[5]

As always, the lesson of history is ambiguous. A certain French philosopher asked himself: if today a Hitler was to come out wanting to publish *Mein Kampf*, ought we allow him to publish it? This is an extreme case. However, one can observe that when *Mein Kampf* was published one could not foresee the likely consequences that would derive from it. Was it not possible that a book so full of logical absurdities and historical inconsistencies would be forgotten in six months?

Tolerance is a method that, as stated, implies the use of persuasion, rather than imposition, towards those who think differently to us. From this point of view, laicism, or a lay mentality, is one of the essential components of the modern world, which even the various religions, in particular Christianity, have ultimately accepted. Such has been the acceptance that the principle of religious freedom, not only of those who profess a religion but also of those who profess none, is affirmed in all modern constitutions.

Notes

1. [Translator's note: Jacques Bossuet (1627–1704) was a French prelate and celebrated pulpit orator, historian, and theological writer.]
2. B. Croce, *Cultura e vita morale* [*Culture and Moral Life*] (Bari, Laterza 1962), p. 100. [Translator's note: In this controversial 1909 (original) article, Croce inveighed against tolerance understood as passive indifference or the outcome of a paralysing relativism.]
3. H. Marcuse, 'Repressive tolerance', in H. Marcuse, R.P. Wolff, and B. Moore Jr, *A Critique of Pure Tolerance* (Boston, Beacon Press 1965), p. 110.
4. G. Mosca, *The Ruling Class* (New York, McGraw-Hill 1939), ch. XV.
5. L. Einaudi 'La parte maggiore e la piu' saggia' ['The greater and wiser number'] in *Il buongoverno* [*Good Government*] (Bari, Laterza 1964), p. 306.

Part IV

For and Against Lay Ethics

Is there a crisis of values?

I state at the outset that my question is not whether today there is a moral crisis, and if so, what is the cause of it. I am neither an historian nor a sociologist. Moreover, I do not have all the necessary data – no one has the necessary data – nor does anyone else, to provide an adequate answer to such an emotionally laden question: 'Is our age experiencing a crisis of values?' This is followed by our need to know where this crisis of values is occurring. In Italy, in Europe, in part of the world, or everywhere? By asking the question in this way, we soon realize how difficult, if not impossible, the answer is. Our evaluations of such a subject are bound to be subjective, since there are chronic pessimists and extreme optimists. As pessimism and optimism are moods, there is no rational argument or empirical observation, even if these could be obtained, that would possibly influence them. There are traditionalists for whom everything in the past was beautiful and, conversely, everything in the present is ugly. Then there are progressivists who project their aspirations into the future instead of retreating into the past. They believe that, despite appearances, our history is inevitably moving towards the betterment of humankind. Finally, there are the discouraged and the trusting, and so on.

The word 'crisis' is more the expression of an inward impulse than of judgement based on arguments derived from either reason or experience. Interestingly, there is no historical period that has not been considered as a period of crisis, from one side or other. I have heard about crises in all the different ages of my life: after World War I, during Fascism and Nazism, during World War II, in the post-war period, and during those years termed *gli anni di piombo* [the years of terrorism]. I have always doubted whether the concept of crisis has any utility in defining a society or even an epoch. Given that we do not have sufficient data to evaluate the present, we would have even less to express a judgement on past epochs, or to make comparisons. Today, moralists argue against hedonism, or hedonistic conception of life (consumerism being its most obvious and significant expression). However, such a strong criticism is valid, if it is at all valid, for only a small section of humanity. How can one speak of hedonism in all those countries where people starve to death or, until recently, in totalitarian states where a seemingly moral discipline was attained at the cost of harsh repression? Every epoch produces its moralists, its preachers, be they religious or lay, who condemn moral corruption, or the unstoppable pleasure-seeking trend, or the search for the ephemeral that proceeds at the same pace as indifference for the eternal. As the saying goes, 'The world is the same all over', to which I would not hesitate to say analogously, 'All history is reflected in the present.'

I doubt whether one could really speak of the moral progress of humanity. At the same time, I doubt that one could plausibly speak of regression. Today we are continually shocked and terrified by all the pervasive violence. In effect, what has changed is the quantity of violence due to significant technological advancement, which has been used to produce increasingly more lethal weapons. Furthermore, the mass media, another outcome of technological progress, enable us to witness daily, rather hourly, violent scenes and conflicts occurring all over the globe, and not just, as was in the past, in neighbouring countries. We have no hesitation in speaking of European or Christian civilization, despite the stark examples of genocide. Some reminders are those of the South American Indians committed by the Spanish, even as subjects of a Catholic King, and of the Indians in North America by the English, who were usually representatives of reformed churches. Then, there were the slave trade of blacks that persisted for centuries, the wars of religion which for decades stained Europe with blood, and the wars for European domination caused by the whim of princes. The Napoleonic wars and finally the two world wars conclude our rapid survey. What could one add about the brutal crimes whose horror defies description in the news of any age? There is also the equally brutal punishment meted out by legitimate governments, for which Michel Foucault provides such a well-documented and forthright description in his *Discipline and Punish*.

Clearly, I do not intend to accuse the past to absolve the present, or deplore the present to praise the good old times. My aim is simply to promote an understanding that any overly assertive judgement in this field runs the risk of being perceived as rash. Certainly, some epochs are more turbulent and others less so. Nevertheless, mindful of our question, it is difficult to say whether the greater turbulence derives from a moral crisis (caused by a diminishing belief in fundamental principles) or from other factors, whether economic, social, political, cultural, or even biological causes.

The two sides of history

Every age presents two sides, and our ability to see either one or the other depends on the position we adopt. Seldom do we manage to adopt a perspective from which both sides can be seen simultaneously. From this arises the extraordinary ambiguity of human history (which after all, corresponds to the inconsistency of human nature), where good and evil are mutually opposed, converge, or become confused. Personally, I have no hesitation in asserting that evil has always prevailed over good, pain over joy, suffering over pleasure, unhappiness over happiness and death over life. Naturally, I cannot provide an explanation for this terrible experience of human history. I withhold any judgement regarding theological explanations. I prefer to say, I do not know. I am unable to answer the distressing question about why we live in this universe. Here (according to Spinoza's classic example) in order to survive the big fish must eat the smaller fish, and the only reason for the little fish to exist seems to be that they are a food resource for the big fish. In my view, the world of humans has not followed a very different course, except that sometimes, by uniting, the smaller fish manage to kill the big fish, but at what significant cost in sacrifices, suffering, and bloodshed! Despite my inability to offer a sensible explanation of what happens and why it does, I can calmly state that the dark dimension of this history is greater than the light.

Nevertheless, I do not deny the existence of a light side (or the other side of the coin). Even today, when our whole history seems threatened with death (hence the claim about a 'second death'),[1] there are some bright moments, which would be unfair to neglect. These are the abolition of slavery, a seemingly irreversible trend, suppression of torture in many countries and, in some others, even of the death penalty. Of course, I cannot forget to mention the emancipation of women, the only true revolution of our time. The greatest victory for a nonviolent society consists of the establishment in many countries of a democratic regime. This is a system that comprises all those institutions which enable an organized group to regulate its coexistence without resorting to violence. Moreover, they allow alternation of the political class without the new side having to eliminate the old physically, as mostly has been the case in history. I refer in passing to Jacques Heers's *Parties and Political Life in the Medieval West*, where in the chapter 'The losers' fate' one reads:

> The end of the fighting, pillaging, arson, massacres, and bestiality merely proclaimed the absolute, insolent triumph of the victorious party. The losers then became the victims of acts of vengeance and violence which were no longer spontaneous outbursts, but rather involved condemnations, various extraordinary measures involving their persons or property and making them outlaws or second-class citizens who were deprived of a substantial part of their political rights.[2]

Among other things, the author relates a passage drawn from Villani's commentary:

And they plucked out the eyes of all the members of the great noble houses of Florence, then beat them to death and threw their bodies into the sea. Only Messer Rinieri Zingane was spared, for he was considered wise and magnanimous. They did not want to kill him, so they merely blinded him, and he finished his days as a monk on the island of Montecristo.[3]

The fear of God

Accordingly, I withhold any judgement on the existence, or otherwise, of a moral crisis. What has certainly changed, or is likely to change progressively in a secularized society (that our society is secularized is a factual judgement whose validity leaves, I believe, few doubts), is how we approach the moral question. To be more precise, it is not so much the question of morality as of moral theory. In a religious society there is no moral theory that can leave out of consideration religious teachings: ethics and religion are inseparable. One of the major arguments to induce individuals to obey moral laws is the fear of God. This is irrespective of whether the argument is advanced with genuine intention by the churches and through their teaching, or instead, whether it is used by the state to achieve its aims, that is, to secure ready obedience to its commands, even those that are unjust. It is an incontestable fact that religion has been the *instrumentum regni* [instrument of rule] that most aptly strengthened the bond between subjects and sovereign. Suffice to recall Machiavelli, whose most significant skill was that of clarity: 'Nor in fact was there ever a legislator who, in introducing extraordinary laws to a people, did not have recourse to God, for otherwise they would not have been accepted. . . . Hence wise men, in order to escape this difficulty, have recourse to God.'[4]

For centuries, even in the modern age and after the advent of the modern state, which is usually held to mark the beginning of the secularization process, the principle of the fear of God as the necessary and unavoidable foundation of morality has remained firm. It therefore follows that moral conduct and the practice of atheism are considered incompatible.

Although well known, it is worth reminding ourselves that one of the staunchest supporters of religious tolerance, John Locke, maintains that atheists must be excluded from tolerance. Let us carefully re-read his words: 'Those are not at all to be tolerated who deny the being of a God.' And what is the reason behind this? The answer is quite clear: 'Promises, covenants, and oaths, which are the bonds of human society, can have no hold upon an atheist. The taking away of God, though but even in thought, dissolves all.'[5]

Today, is there anyone still prepared to maintain such a restrictive thesis? I am certainly not saying that there might not be someone who will. But in effect none of the existing constitutions in liberal democratic or lay states (meaning by this, non-confessional states) upholds that limitation. This is because religious liberty also includes the freedom not to profess any religion. Simply put, this means that tolerance is also extended to atheists. What explanation can we give for this extension? Is it a greater laxity, understood as the diminishing belief in the validity of strict moral rules, which are obligatory for any individual and citizen? Is it the conviction that morals are not necessarily dependent on religion, and atheists can also be moral persons? To give an example close to home, I recall that the only restriction provided by the Italian Constitution (article 19) refers to rituals that are contrary to common decency. It is a limitation that concerns, if anything, certain religions or religious sects, and does not affect those who do not profess a religion since they usually would not practise any rituals. If such a principle has been established, it is so to the extent that it no longer allows any distinction between believers and non-believers for the right to profess their faith (and therefore faith in a universe without God). If that is the case, what is the reason other than the principle, established during the extended process of secularization, according to which obedience to moral laws can be justified without the need to accept God's existence? In other words, are there certain coherent, rational, or reasonable lay morals which are self-sustaining and need no other buttresses than those very human pillars of reason and experience?

Four attempts at establishing lay morals

Beginning with natural law theory, the history of modern ethics represents an attempt, or rather a series of attempts, to establish objective ethics. They are also termed rational or empirical, or can at the same time be rational and empirical. In short, they are lay, or secular, ethics. There is a need to understand if, and to what extent, these attempts have succeeded because, undoubtedly, today the debate about the different solutions is still raging as tenaciously as ever. The same uncertainty persists in the conclusions used to oppose the different types of ethics from the beginning of Western philosophy to the present. One need only consider the clash between Epicureanism and Stoicism, or between the ethics of virtue and the ethics of happiness, and so on.

Here certainly is not the place to review the whole history of this old debate, even if I were able. However, it seems to me that in the modern age, four significant moral theories, together with their relative sub-theories, can be identified. These are based on those arguments so far advanced to establish lay or non-confessional ethics, which are not linked to a religious faith, and hence also bind atheists.

The first and also the most widespread of these is natural law theory. Of course, I mean the modern version that begins with Grotius's well-known statement[6] (in §11 of the 'Prolegomena' to *The Rights of War and Peace*). Accordingly, natural laws are valid *etiamsi daremus non esse Deum aut non curari ab eo negotia humana* [even if we were to grant that God does not exist or human affairs are not in his care] (a renowned but not original formula because, as is well documented, the same formula was expounded by earlier theologians, such as Gregorio da Rimini and Gabriel Biel). The objections advanced against natural law theory are twofold:

1 The ambiguity of the concept of human nature, which has been assigned a different meaning by the various authors. For example, as negative by Hobbes for whom individuals are bellicose by nature, and positive by Rousseau for

whom individuals are peaceful by nature. Moreover, the most diverse institutions (for example, individual and collective property, liberty and slavery etc.) are considered institutions of natural law, since they are consistent with human nature.

2   Even supposing that human nature was an open book and could be easily read, it must still be demonstrated that all that is natural is good simply because it is natural. Such evidence cannot be provided unless it is assumed that nature stems from goodwill, and in this way one reintroduces a theological and fideistic argument that frustrates and precludes the rationalist assumption.

The deductive process of natural law supporters is contrasted with the inductive process intrinsic to ethics, whose fundamental argument to support the objectivity of value judgement rests in *consensus humani generis* [the consensus of humankind]. Or stated differently, this is the factual or historical observation that a certain rule of behaviour is common among all peoples. Aristotle's statement, in the Fifth Book of *Nicomachean Ethics*, that natural law is operative everywhere, strengthens this type of argument. Even for this moral theory there are two main objections:

1   Are there really universal laws, or laws that are valid 'everywhere', in every nation, and have always been effective (universal not only in space but also in time)? The most sensational example is the principle 'Do not kill', which is usually valid within the group, save in exceptional instances similar to that of legitimate defence. This, however, does not generally apply in relations between groups, where every individual behaviour is always subject to the principle *salus rei publicae suprema lex* [the security of the state is the supreme law].

2   Although there are laws that have been in force for centuries, this fact alone does not mean they can be accepted as moral rules. Here a most outstanding example is slavery. One of the weakest arguments advanced by supporters of abortion during the referendum campaign in 1981

was that based on the assumption that abortion has always been practised. Even if it could be proven that an overwhelming majority of women always accepted this practice, this is not a good reason to consider it morally right. This also applies to the death penalty. Not only has this always been practised, and not only does it still persist in quite a number of states today, but it was also defended by eminent thinkers, from Plato to Hegel.

The third of the moral theories is the Kantian, usually also referred to as formal or formalistic. This is because what ought to be done or not is established by a purely formal criterion, such as the ability of an action to become universal, which Kant formulates thus: 'Act in such a way that you can wish your maxim to become a universal law.' He uses the promise as an example: if I make a promise with no intention of maintaining it, can I expect such a failure to become a universal law? Clearly, Kant is not a utilitarian, and therefore does not assert the utility or convenience of maintaining promises, by arguing that if one does not keep the promise one risks being repaid in kind, and thus could suffer some harm. According to Kant, it is not out of caution that one must keep promises, since in certain instances it would be more sensible not to keep them. For Kant there is another reason, and this is logical rather than empirical. If I elevate the failure to keep promises to a universal principle, I aspire to a world where making promises would no longer make sense. As Kant states: 'As soon as my principle became a universal law it would self-destruct.'

I express two objections to the Kantian argument:

1   The fact that I do not aspire to a world where promises are not kept derives from the negative value judgement I give of such a world. But in this way, even Kantian ethics become teleological. That is, they are ethics whose validity depends on the merit of the aim (a society where promises will be kept). Teleological ethics are no longer simply formal, and hence lose the universal character they derived from their claimed formalism.

2   Is it possible for two actions that obey the same criterion, which considers them capable of becoming universal, to be incompatible? If this is the case, which action should be chosen? Let us consider two fundamental rules of behaviour present in every civilized society: 'Do not use violence against your equals' and 'Prevent the violent from overwhelming the nonviolent' (or if you wish the strong from oppressing the weak). Both principles are consistent with the criterion of universalizability. In effect, I cannot aspire to either a world where mutual violence is legitimate, which would inevitably lead to the Hobbesean 'war of all against all', or a world where the arrogant prevail. But rarely can the two principles be observed contemporaneously. The same can be said of maintaining promises. I cannot aspire to a world where promises are not kept. But can I desire a world where a hired killer keeps the promise to carry out the murder, to which he has agreed with other accomplices? The same difficulty emerges concerning the principle 'Do not lie'. Even this restraint is not absolute. Suffice to think of the case of a compassionate lie (coherently rejected by Kant), or of the more sensational case of a rebel who is caught, and who by lying saves his companions still at large. (Today, is there anyone who does not feel a sense of moral revulsion for the *pentiti* [repentant criminals] who betray their cohorts? Yet they tell the truth, and in addition their evidence assists the state.)

The fourth set of ethics consists of utilitarianism. Today, this is the most widely debated, at least in the Anglo-Saxon world and by extension in Italy. The accepted facts, on which utilitarianism is based are the feelings of pleasure or pain. From this emerges the thesis according to which the criterion for differentiating right from wrong rests in the degree of pleasure and pain respectively that an action produces. However, utilitarianism as an ethical theory encounters numerous difficulties. The first consists of the calculation of pleasure and pain, compounded by the fact that for Bentham, in addition to quantity one should also measure the intensity, the duration, the certainty, the proximity, the richness, and the purity of pleasure and pain. But before all these characteristics can be arranged hierarchically, they need to be compared with each other. But which is the preferred order: an intense but brief pleasure, or a less intense pleasure with a longer duration? A further difficulty rests in the relation that necessarily must be established between my pleasure (or pain) and that experienced by others. Because humans live together in society, a single individual cannot be isolated from all the others, and therefore one cannot leave out of consideration the effects that the fulfilment of my happiness has on the enjoyment of the happiness of others. But who are these others? My neighbours, my fellow citizens, all living beings on this earth, only those now living or also future generations? There is a rather disappointing vagueness about Bentham's principle of 'the happiness of the greater number'. Was extermination of six million Jews necessary for the happiness of the Germans, who certainly were a 'greater number'? Now, it is easy for us to say the extermination did not benefit the Germans, who, in spite of that, lost the war. But what if they had won? Finally, a particularly widespread objection to utilitarianism is that raised by those who consider justice the primary good of human society, meaning by this a just distribution of resources within a particular organized group. How is a just distribution of wealth or services established on the basis of utilitarian criteria? The criteria that usually inspire distributive justice, such as merit, ability, or need, are not utilitarian.

It is true that all these difficulties (and others) caused a number of utilitarians to advocate a new form of utilitarianism, which unlike traditional utilitarianism, or act utilitarianism, is known as rules utilitarianism. According to this perspective, the question is no longer what action, but what rule, is more useful. A solution of this kind claims to avoid some *aporie*, or paradoxes, of direct utilitarianism, since by adopting the viewpoint of the utility of the rule, for example, 'Do not lie', utility is proportional to the benefits derived from the existence of this rule. This is also valid when, in a particular case, from the perspective of active utilitarianism telling the truth could have worse consequences than not telling it. However, it is noted that ultimately rules utilitarianism cannot on the one hand avoid the utility criterion, even if it is applied to the rule, and therefore to the difficulties of utilitarianism in general. Resolution is achieved through completely different ethics, that is, deontological ethics. In this case, conforming to the rule is optimal, irrespective of the judgement of the consequences. Moreover, judgement of the consequences is the characteristic of utilitarianism, as opposed to all the theories for which judgement of right and wrong derives exclusively from the existence of rules.

But are religious ethics a solution?

As can be seen, none of the most common theories of morals is free from criticisms. It seems, therefore, that every attempt to provide a rational foundation for moral principles is likely to fail. Nowadays, the debate among moral philosophers has become increasingly subtle, but the result does not change. They use the most refined techniques of logical reasoning, but the schools contesting the field for one solution to prevail over the other conduct a complicated game of 'for and against' that becomes confused in an endless tangle.

In recent years, in the face of this persistent opposition, three possible solutions have reappeared with a certain frequency:

1   the appeal to evidence or ethical intuition;
2   the absolute relativism intrinsic to the so-called 'non-cognitivist' moral theories, where value judgements are expressions of emotions, feelings, personal preferences, or options, with one being as valid as the other;
3   the sphere of moral judgements is the sphere not of the rational but of the reasonable, where arguments inherent to rhetoric, or the art of persuasion, as distinct from logic or demonstrative art, apply.

Of these three solutions, the first surpasses reason: it is ultra-rational. The second represses reason, considering it completely useless: it is infra-rational. The third limits its possibilities, maintaining that one can reason on the subject of morals but can never reach the ultimate foundations through reason: it is quasi-rational.

The problematic nature of rational ethics rekindles the need to base ethics on religion, and strengthens the assertion according to which there are no ethics independent of religion. But then, are we so certain that religious ethics will not meet the same objections as those directed at classical theories of ethics within the ambits of reason only? There are two possible cases. The first is where religious ethics are reduced to the theory of what is known as theological voluntarism, and accordingly what God commands is just, and what he prohibits is unjust. This produces a type of juridification of ethics consistent with the maxim *auctoritas non veritas facit legem* [authority not truth makes the law]. Consequently, every action, even the most ruthless and inhumane, can be justified by the plea that 'God wills it.' History has shown us the grim effects produced by religious fanaticism. The other case is based on the thesis according to which it is not what God commands that is just, but that God commands what is just (this is the classic argument of Euthyphro). Here, the criterion of what is just or unjust is not God's will but his nature, which being essentially good can only prescribe good actions. However, this is a perfectly circular answer. What other argument do we have to define God as essentially good, except for the proof that actions prescribed by him are good? The only way out of this circle is to renounce ethical voluntarism and embrace 'theological rationalism'. According to this, actions prescribed by God are good, not because they are prescribed, but because they are intrinsically good (in and of themselves). But theological rationalism meets the same objections and encounters the same aporias as does every form of ethical rationalism. To begin with, there is no form of rationalism whose moral precept is valid in every circumstance, and does not allow for exceptions, as indicated by the formulae: 'You must not kill, but...'; 'You must not lie but...'; 'You must keep promises but...'. Ultimately, the choice of acting according to the general rule or not depends on a calculation of the consequences. As already stated this can only lead to probable solutions that are entrusted to the judgement of individual conscience. But a probabilistic solution is such that it will dissolve any claim by theological ethics of being absolute (or, more certain than worldly ethics). In other words, if it is true that every rule implies some exceptions, and does not apply in all possible cases, judgement of the probable exceptionality is derived from two means. The first is the will of God, who in that particular circumstance commanded the rule be violated, and thus one reverts to theological voluntarism. Alternatively, one is forced through debate to resort to subjects such as nature, consensus, the criterion of universalizability, and utility. However, as we have seen, these usually lead to disputable results. Furthermore, they transform the moral imperative from the categorical ('You must') to the hypothetical ('You must, unless the condition is such as to allow derogation from the general principle').

The real problem is compliance

Having said this, the discussion is not yet over. The profound reason for linking morals to a religious vision of the world rests not so much on the need to establish morals as on the practically more important need for compliance. What is absolutely necessary for any kind of human coexistence is not only the existence of well-established rules of behaviour, but also compliance with them. Jurists differentiate between the validity and the efficacy of a rule. By transposing this expression to moral theory we can say that it is not sufficient for the existence of rules to be proven, that is their validity, but it is also necessary for the established rules to be observed effectively. From this, then, it can be seen how the plea to God usually serves, and does so quite well, not so much to justify the existence of obligatory rules of behaviour as to induce the recipients of those rules not to violate them. In short, that plea is directed to God as the (infallible) judge and stern executioner against transgression, rather than to God as legislator. The well-known maxim 'If there is no God, every-thing is allowed'[7] can mean two different things: (1) if there is no God there are no criteria on which to differentiate right from wrong, and the criteria usually exhibited are uncertain, ineffectual, and fallible; (2) if there is no God, individuals cannot be induced to observe moral laws. To know about moral law and to observe it are two completely different things, and the latter does not necessarily follow from the former. If we return for a moment to the reason advanced by Locke to exclude atheists from tolerance, we realize that the reason for that exclusion does not rest in the fact that atheists are unaware of moral laws. Rather, because their behaviour cannot be influenced by the fear of God, they cannot provide any guarantee that they will honour their word, or feel bound by any oath. In other words, atheists are a threat to the stability of a republic because they do not fear God's punish-ment. Since they lack this fear, they can be less disposed to observe moral laws, which impose sacrifices, limit the sphere of desires, and oblige one to place duty before pleasure.

By this I mean that the limits of ethical rationalism are even more evident when the subject of the foundations of morals is renounced, and we confront the practically more important subject of the implementation of moral laws. To demonstrate the validity of a rule, a good reason can be sufficient. But this same good reason is usually not enough for it to be observed. The subject of the foundations of moral laws is as theoretic-ally absorbing as it is practically irrelevant. There is no moral principle that is observed for the simple fact that it is well founded. The philosophical debate on morals, on which I dwelled, is a theoretical debate, an admirable intellectual game that has little or limited impact on real attitudes. Moral reasoning is valid for that small minority of individuals who allow themselves to be guided by reason and persuaded by good arguments. The typical rational argument, 'Do not do unto others what you would not like done unto you', is useless to someone who thinks, for example, that if he does not follow this principle but everyone else does, no harm will come to him, and very little to society. Likewise, if I steal, assuming that no one else does, I can happily continue to steal. If I do not keep promises, assuming that others do, I can persist in not keeping them with my maximum advantage and minimum disadvantage for society.

To achieve compliance with major moral principles there is a need for much more than their rational justification. Historical experience reveals that it is necessary to threaten such punishments as will discourage violation of established rules. At this point, law enters the scene as a coercive system. But even more so, it is the fear of God that has always been considered a no less intense form of intimidation, and sometimes more intense than legal threat. It is difficult to comprehend Locke's intolerance towards atheists if one is not persuaded that the fear of God (of divine justice, strengthened by severe sanctions, compared with which human punishments are like a mother's spankings) is a good reason, rather the best of reasons, to ensure obedience to moral laws. Only from this perspective can one presume that in a secular society, moral laws are less observed than in a religious one, and therefore the average standard of morality is less widespread. But is this a valid argument to demonstrate the existence of God or the truth of Christianity? I maintain that no profoundly religious man, no Christian would be prepared to base the truth of his religion, or of Christianity, solely on the validity and efficacy of morals that derive from them. Is this not a way that might lead one to accept a religious belief for pragmatic reasons? Would we not run, once again, into a vicious circle? One would end basing the validity of religion on morals, whereas religion, if it is true and assuming that it is, should be the basis for morals. How do we exit this vicious circle? Through an act of faith? But it was precisely the attitude of faith that one wanted to avoid by deducing the truth of Christianity from the necessity to provide a foundation to morals.

'Superbe fole'

I must confess that I hesitate to enter the great jungle of philosophic debate about the relations between faith and reason. I am not so personally confident that I will not risk getting lost, losing my fellow explorers as well. However, I think that it can be deduced from what I have stated thus far that, if today one can witness a religious revival, this emerges out of moral discomfort. The non-believer must honestly realize that there are 'limits to ethical rationalism', which echoes the title of a work by Erminio Juvalta, a University of Turin scholar, and a dear friend. Humans cannot avoid reasoning, but reason alone is not enough. Followers of reason alone know their limits, and they are precluded from going beyond them. At most, they endeavour to glimpse a world where humans have matured to the extent that they are capable of judging right from wrong through their own strength of conviction (according to Kant's essay on the Enlightenment, they have come of age). Moreover, to know what they must do, and above all to do it effectively, they do not need any other teachings than those of reason and experience.

They would not be men and women of reason, however, if they did not doubt the advent of this other world, which moreover in our age of armed conflict and devastation appears more distant than ever. They would not be men and women of reason if they were so confident, so presumptuous and arrogant that they could herald a world in which, to repeat the words of the most despondent poet in Italy's history:

Justice and piety shall find a different soil
Than those proud follies [*superbe fole*], founded upon which
The probity of the mob
Stands firm as all things else rooted in error.[8]

Notes

1. J. Schell, *The Fate of the Earth* (London, Picador 1982).
2. J. Heers, *Parties and Political Life in the Medieval West* (Amsterdam, North-Holland 1977), p. 177.
3. Ibid., p. 178.
4. N. Machiavelli, *The Discourses of Niccolò Machiavelli* (London, Routledge 1975), I.11.4.

5. J. Locke, *A Letter Concerning Toleration* (The Hague, Martinus Nijhoff 1963), p. 93.

6. Hugo Grotius, *The Rights of War and Peace* (London, Boothroyd 1814), p. 22.

7. I point out that the opposite maxim, 'If God exists (and this means God is with me), everything is allowed', could be elevated as a principle of the opposite conception to nihilism, which is fundamentalism.

8. Giacomo Leopardi, *Selected Prose and Poetry*, ed., trans., and intro. Iris Origo and John Heath-Stubbs (New York, New American Library 1967), pp. 279–80. [Translator's note: The quotation is from his 'La ginestra' ('The broom', or 'The flower of the desert'), v. 153–5. Bobbio cites vs. 153–4. 'Superbe' is to be understood as a sign of arrogance or haughtiness, and 'fole' as illusions or useless fantasies.]

The Gods that Failed

Some questions on the problem of evil

The events in Sarajevo,[1] when considered from different perspectives, say, of the ethical, or of political opportunity, or of economic convenience itself, surpass the threshold of what is comprehensible. Beyond this, the question that inevitably emerges concerns the invincible presence of Evil in the world. It is one of those questions that we are unable to answer through the wisdom of our reason, and for which we use the sibylline term, 'metaphysical'.

The question of Evil dominates our attention with particular force in the case of disastrous events, irrespective of whether the protagonists are Nature or History. In our most recent memory there are two events that have promoted considerable debate on the topic: Auschwitz and the fall of the Berlin Wall. The first represented a challenge, above all, to the man of faith, the other, above all, to the man of reason. Two questions resounded repeatedly in our ears: 'Why has God not only been silent, but also allowed an outrageous massacre, unprecedented in history for both the number of victims and the cruelty of the means adopted, to be perpetrated?'; and 'Why has the greatest movement that claimed to emancipate humanity from domination, exploitation and alienation overturned into its opposite, that is, into a politically despotic, economically inefficient and morally despicable state?' Men of reason are tempted to speak of 'God's defeat', and men of faith to speak of 'the suicide of revolution'.

In reality, it is not only men of faith who, confronted with the disastrous outcome of the Communist Revolution, spoke of 'the upturned utopia'. Equally, it has not been only men of reason who spoke about 'the defeat of God'. When I read Sergio Quinzio's book with precisely this title,[2] I was flabbergasted. As a non-believer, who despite everything continues to remain at the threshold, I would never have imagined that a man of faith could be so outspoken about the failure of Christianity that has not kept its promises, and about the defeat of the Crucifix. The story of God is from the first pages of the Bible 'a history of defeats': 'After two thousand years the dead have not risen, and the space given to faith has diminished tremendously'; 'We can no longer believe in a God that demands an infinite price in blood and tears to provide a solution that no one has yet seen'; 'God who sacrificed himself for us, and expects salvation from us, is a God we should love totally, but He has made us too weary, disillusioned, and unhappy to be able to do so.'

Over past decades, there have been analogous, and no less sincere, mournful disapprovals, bitter reflections, and self-critical confessions about the unborn 'new man', and the old who not only is not dead but survives, although in a worse state than before. We have read these expressions a thousand times in connection with the other significant failure, the Communist Revolution, considered magnificent for the sheer numbers involved, and in good faith judged grand by millions of people for the aim it proposed.

It seems, therefore, that for the believer the failure of God proceeded simultaneously with the failure of reason for the non-believer, and that both contribute to our inability to maintain any illusions about the advancing age of nihilism. Many of us who experienced fascism and communism would remember a collection of essays with the title *Il Dio che ha fallito* [*The God that Failed*], edited by Ignazio Silone, on the October Revolution, and about the hopes that it raised and were subsequently frustrated. But now there is someone that seems to be prompting us to ask: 'Which God?'

Nevertheless, we cannot place the two failures on the same level, comparing them, and drawing the same consequences from both of them. Men of reason have always suspected, although not openly professed, the possibility of error, admitting the insufficiency of their knowledge without divine help, and leaving the way open for continuous revision of their claims. For believers, is not the defeat of God a more disturbing, and above all a more disastrous, event? Trust in reason has never been as absolute as trust in divine providence. We never had difficulty in accepting reason as becoming rather than being. Now we learn that even God is not projected in History, but becomes. What is the difference, then, between this God who becomes in History, and the Reason of philosophers, or Hegel's Spirit? We also read that God 'suffers'. God is not omnipotent, and this is why he suffers. If he were omnipotent he would not have allowed Auschwitz. Is it no longer God who saves us, but we who must save God? Is a kind of weak theology becoming evident in an anguished society, which is strangely finding its place beside the so-called philosophical 'feebleness'? How short is the distance to reach the radical overturning of the traditional vision of the universe, according to which God is the creator and a human being the creature, into the humanistic and similarly radical vision according to which God is the creation of a human being? Is there no longer the human being depicted in the Bible as being created in the image and likeness of God, but this new God, who is not but becomes, no longer omnipotent but impotent and fallible, created in the image and likeness of the human being?

From the analytical perspective I propose to present some reflections without any pretence except to ask some of the many questions that I ask myself. Thus, continuing the discussion I begin with a fundamental distinction: Evil has two aspects. Although these are often and not always reasonably connected, they must be kept quite distinct. They are active Evil and passive Evil. The first is that which is committed, the other is that which is sustained. In other words, inflicted Evil and endured Evil. Within the general concept of evil we understand two opposed human realities, wickedness and suffering. Two paradigmatic figures of these two sides of evil are Cain and Job. When we pose the question of evil in general, as we are presently doing, our mind races indifferently to either a violent episode or a painful one. This could be depicted both by the image of a ruthless murderer, and by that of a crying mother. In evoking Sarajevo we see fleeting images of soldiers firing, of executioners and victims, and of panic-stricken men and women escaping. These images alternate with each other, become superimposed on each other, and become continuously confused with each other.

I would like to stress that in common understanding the passive meaning prevails over the active. In our everyday language, expressions such as 'I feel unwell', 'It hurts so badly', 'I have a headache', 'Why are you hurting me?', all refer to passive evil. Does not our way of speaking reveal that our experience of suffering is much broader than that of wickedness? I would be inclined to answer yes. Active evil, in the form of will to power, abuse, and violence in all its forms, from an individual murder to a massacre, is a particular subject of reflection, above all for historians, theologians, philosophers, and those who question themselves about 'Evil in the world'. Instead, suffering belongs to everyone. It remains hidden but is more widespread, and is less visible precisely because it is deeper. The pain of living evades History, on whose stage those who usually appear are the powerful, the conquerors, those who use violence more than those who have experienced violence, and the masters more than the slaves.

This first observation helps me to correct an error, or perhaps more than an error. This is the mental habit that consists of connecting inflicted evil to endured evil, as if they existed in an interdependent relationship. Such a mental habit derives from the non-reflective acceptance of one of the classic arguments, so widespread as to have become popular, advanced both to justify and to alleviate suffering: that suffering is the consequence of guilt. The model for this interpretation is to be sought in the daily life of any human society. There, in order for a peaceful coexistence to be possible, one of the fundamental rules that must be observed establishes that crime must be followed by punishment. Those who have killed must be killed. Those who have inflicted suffering must suffer. From this perspective, suffering is always a punishment, in the sense implied by the term 'punishment' in a retributive conception of justice. If there is suffering, that implies there was an offence. Active and passive evil constitute an indissoluble unity, but the active comes first, then the passive. The latter would not occur unless the former preceded it. I point out that the term 'punishment' has two fundamental meanings: of sanction of a violent act, and of suffering that can be sustained irrespective of having committed a cruel act. This second meaning also reveals the existence of that vast domain of human experience where passive evil exists without it necessarily being dependent on active evil. The fact that a punishment makes one suffer does not imply that the condition of suffering is also a punishment as sanction for a crime. The verb 'to suffer', as with the adjective 'painful', does not have any relationship with punishment understood as sanction. Punishment can be painful, but the painfulness is not necessarily related to a punishment.

From daily reality the principle of retributive justice, or the necessary relation between inflicted evil and sustained evil, is transferred within archaic societies to the interpretation of the entire universe. I am referring to what has been called 'the socio-morphic model'. That is to say, it concerns that mental operation through which the entire system of the universe is depicted as an imitation of the social system and of the rules that govern it. Even the passive evil in the universe, the dreadful suffering of humankind throughout its history, would be nothing more than the inevitable and unavoidable consequence of an active original evil, the initial notion of which has been forgotten, but the knowledge of which is steeped in a mythical past, and the memory of which is transmitted from generation to generation. What occurs in the universe, which includes all humans who have lived, all those actually living, and all those who will live in centuries to come, is no different from what occurs in the small society in which we live. Active evil would precede the passive, once again a crime would occur before the penalty, and sin be committed before punishment. Humans would not be suffering if the first person had not sinned. Even the whole universe in its overall spatiality and temporaneity would be governed as always and for ever, according to the fundamental principle of retributive justice. It has been observed, but it is a subject on which I cannot dwell, that one of the features of the pre-scientific mentality, when confronted with an unfamiliar event, is to ask oneself the question: 'Whose fault is it?' rather than: 'What is the cause?'

Even today, in the vision of a popular religion, and not limited to that, the interpretation of the universe according to the principle of retributive justice is predominant. The fact that suffering, any suffering, in some way discharges a debt serves not only as explanation, the easiest of explanations, but also as justification, the most appeasing of justifications. It is common too, and not without the direct support of traditional theodicy, whose major and most persistently recurrent argument to justify the event that causes suffering is to ascribe it to some presumed human guilt, and thus absolve divine power. It is of no concern that the offender remains unknown. The fact that there is a guilty party is the logical deduction from the principle of retributive justice, set axiomatically as the regulative principle of the universe. One can make the most diverse and peculiar hypotheses on the nature of guilt and of the offender. The only issue that it would seem cannot be disputed is, I repeat once again, that if a punishment exists, there must have been an offence.

According to the rule of individual responsibility, it does not even matter that the punishment affects the presumed offender. The principle of retributive justice, which is applied not to the offence for a single crime, but to an offence that affects a group of individuals at a particular time in history and in a particular society, leaves completely out of consideration the rule of individual responsibility. To illustrate with the usual examples, a new disease, such as the plague was in ancient times, or syphilis at the end of the fifteenth century, and AIDS today, although less convincingly following the advancement of the secularization process. Wherever the principle of collective guilt is effective, it is immaterial to know the single offender. In a primitive conception of justice there is no reason for which the punishment should only affect the offender, and only the guilty party should suffer the penalty. In a global vision of justice and of the universe, it is absolutely irrelevant that a single individual, or a group of individuals, or an entire population, should suffer for an offence they did not commit.

Until such time as there is a nexus between evil and human action, such as in the cases so far advanced, the cause of retributive justice can still be upheld, although somewhat imperfectly. Thus, humans in general are responsible for all actions by humankind. Humanity can be conceived as an undifferentiated totality, in which every part of the whole is responsible for what it does with respect to the others. But does the reason for human suffering derive solely from human causes? I stated at the outset that the sphere of passive evil is incomparably larger than that of active evil. It is a fact that human suffering can derive from endless other causes that do not depend on our action, whether voluntary or involuntary. Rather, the overwhelming majority of conditions of suffering cannot be attributed to our guilt, beginning, above all, with the reason for pain, or the death of loved ones. As far as it concerns us personally, more than the thought of our death, the main cause of suffering is illness, both physical and psychological. Once again, the majority of these do not derive from our mistakes or guilt. Where does the long and often terrible suffering of a cancer patient come from? Can it ever be attributed to anyone? What can one say of hereditary illnesses? What would be the sense in attempting to trace them back, even if it were possible, to the original ancestor? They are absurd questions to ill-founded problems. Absurd, precisely because the questions are ill-founded.

The major challenge to the comfortable solution that sees a nexus between suffering and guilt, and which therefore believes it is capable of solving the problem in the human domain, is natural disasters. This is so well known by theologians that they cannot abandon the idea of divine providence. It is equally well understood by philosophers of history who substitute divine providence with reasoning. There is no significant natural disaster that has not raised its question of 'why'. I mean by this the theological 'why', since the causal 'why' can probably have an answer. But it is a problem that from the viewpoint of any theodicy or logodicy is insoluble, despite the subtle arguments advanced to confront it, and the ingenuousness employed in attempting to resolve it. Yet it is natural disasters, such as earthquakes, floods, cyclones, and hurricanes, that cause the greatest amount of suffering in the shortest time, a number of dead, of wounded, and of material losses that the scourge of war generated over longer periods. If one assesses both the depth of evil, and time duration when the evil occurred, natural disasters are the most terrifying evidence of Evil as suffering. It is an evil that cannot be subjected in any way to the comfortable, and comforting, justifications of the necessary relationship between guilt and punishment.

No one possesses such a capacity for compassion as to be able to suffer together with all the victims of an event. That is, to be capable of drawing to oneself the overall pain felt by the survivors of a family buried under the rubble, or of the homeless, or those who witnessed the destruction in an instant of everything they possessed. Justification of suffering through guilt is so entrenched in our mentality that even in the case of an earthquake there is no lack of outcry, though quite understandable, against those responsible for bad regional policy. The hunt for a scapegoat is one way of externalizing one's pain and indignation. If there is a responsible party, that means there is someone on whom to take revenge, and who can be made to suffer as we did. But the first link in the chain is nevertheless always a natural event, whose devastating consequences can be increased, of course, but cannot be considered the exclusive effect of human negligence. Any inquiry undertaken on the responsibility of public administrations always remains a vast disproportion compared with the damages produced by the disaster, that is, between the first cause and the secondary causes. It is a disparity that no argument of justification, even the most elaborate, can bridge.

A natural disaster is a fact, and as such can only be explained by the same mental processes by which any fact is explained. In a theological or moral conception of the world, we can say absolutely nothing on the meaning of such a fact, since we are not certain that there is a subject to whom it can be attributed. Let us compare an earthquake to a war. The comparison is possible because both are events that generate an unprecedented amount of suffering. But here the comparison ends. Let us attempt the comparison at the level of moral judgement. While it makes sense to speak, as has been done for centuries, of a just and unjust war, it would be meaningless to speak of a just or unjust earthquake. But it is understandable that in a theodicy or logodicy, that is to say, in terms of a discussion in which there is an assumption that there is a subject to whom Good and Evil can be attributed, the argument is plausible.

To add to the difficulty, not to say the impossibility, of turning a natural disaster into an event to be justified on the basis of a moral criterion, there is the observation that some of these disasters, such as earthquakes, floods, in particular volcanic eruptions, nearly always occur in the same areas, while others are unaffected by them. Since Aristotle's time, there are essentially two forms of justice: commutative and distributive. A classic example of commutative justice is Evil-punishment, as remedy for Evil-guilt. This form of justice is violated when suffering, as in natural disasters, is without guilt. Wherever there is good without merit or evil without guilt, the principle of distributive justice should intervene, according to which Good and Evil must be equitably distributed. But there is no theodicy or logodicy that can justify the repetitiveness of devastating events in the same parts of the world. Besides, even in the case where the event occurs in a certain location for the first time, the question is still asked: 'Why just there, and not elsewhere?' Therefore, if any discussion of justification cannot be related to either of the two forms of justice, the commutative or the distributive, it must be concluded that there is no decisive argument that we can advance to justify those events which, more than any other, because of their seriousness, would require justification.

I do not propose to enter into a discussion on the cruelty, and correspondingly, on the suffering, in the animal world where the most ruthless struggles for survival occur.

According to Spinoza's famous example, the big fish eats the small fish, and the small fish seems to have no reason to exist other than to be eaten, and thus enable the big fish not to starve to death. Those who may have watched those frequent television programmes in which a snake slowly swallows its victim, destined to die after long suffering; or a lion with bloodstained jaws tears apart a gazelle; or a pack of hungry wolves chases a herd of musk deer, and when one is subdued kill and devour it; cannot avoid asking the question: 'Who wanted such a cruel world?'[3] Is this, then, not a world in which, if there is evolution, this has nothing to do with moral progress, which we talk about when we consider what meaning to attribute to the course of human history? Lay or secular thought refrains from answering these ultimate questions, but rather attempts to explain them based on the causes. An example used is the theory of the struggle for survival, be this explanation good or bad. While lay thought can accept the world of facts for what they are, religious thought cannot. How could it, if the traditional schema of justification, the relationship between guilt and punishment, does not apply outside the human world, where it is presumed humans are free to choose between right and wrong? One of the strong arguments in religious thought is that between God and Evil there is the human being, who has freedom, a tendency towards evil, and other passions. How can such an argument be used to understand the non-human world, where what happens is neither the work of humans, nor influenced by them, other than in a very small way?

Confronted with the problem of Evil, theological thought has an obligation that lay thought does not have. That is to reconcile the presence of Evil with the existence of God, and with the image of God not only as infinite Power, but also as infinite Goodness, of which Evil is the negation.

Relevant to this point is the well-known passage in the essay 'The concept of God after Auschwitz' where Hans Jonas argues that God's three attributes, absolute goodness, absolute power, and intelligibility, cannot be conceived together. This is because 'they stand in such a logical relation to one another that the conjunction of any two of them excludes the third'.[4] In his view, God's omnipotence can only coexist with absolute divine goodness at the cost of God's total unintelligibility, that is, of the conception of God as absolute mystery. 'Only a completely unintelligible God can be said to be absolutely good and absolutely powerful, yet tolerate the world as it is.' In the face of this aporia, Jonas proposes the following. Having to forego one of the three attributes this should be omnipotence, since goodness cannot be separated from our concept of God, and cannot be subjected to any limitation. Knowledge of God is a fundamental element of Judaism, for which the concept of a completely hidden God is unacceptable.

I am wondering whether a solution of this kind may make an alternative solution plausible, at least as a mental experiment. Since the attribute of absolute goodness does make God intelligible, but raises the question of justification of Evil, we could try to reject the attribute of absolute goodness and accept that of absolute power. In this case, God's intelligibility would be saved at the cost of his goodness. But is this perhaps not one of the possible answers of secular humanism, according to which, because God is absolute power, he would be indifferent to Good and Evil, or above Good and Evil, as well as beyond the Beautiful and the Ugly? From this point of view, Good and Evil would be no more than human creations. Moreover, the fact that they are human creations would explain why they do not have an absolute value. On one side, there would not be such a radical atheism as to deny God-power. On the other, there would be such an equally radical humanism as to consider values an exclusive product of history.

One final question. Up to this point I have dwelt mainly on the aporia encountered by the justification of Evil from the perspective of a conception of the universe governed by a principle of retributive justice. But of all the aporias that the problem of Evil submits to our reason, the one considered thus far is not the only one. There is yet another even more disturbing, and for this very reason, more outrageous. Not only, as we have seen, is there no way to demonstrate that behind a punishment there is some guilt, but neither can it be demonstrated that in the universe's general economy the wicked are those who suffer the most. The unpredictabilities of human history can demonstrate, to those who are prepared to evaluate them objectively, exactly the opposite. For instance, the tyrant Stalin died in his bed, while Anne Frank, the image of innocence, died in an extermination camp. Job's plea of 'Why?' is also the question the afflicted have always asked. Is there any reason why the wicked survive and the innocent perish?

Is there any sense in asking the question, which nevertheless at the time disturbed us? Why, at the last moment, did the officer in Hitler's group unwittingly shift the bag containing the bomb that Colonel von Stauffenberg brought with him to make an attempt on Hitler's life, and Hitler went unharmed? He not only survived, but subsequently exacted his brutal revenge.

No, it makes no sense. Even this is a question without answer. But as always the humble person has already provided the answer: 'In this world there is no justice.'

Notes

1. [Translator's note: During the Bosnian war, Sarajevo was subjected to incessant military bombardments and other atrocities, such as that on Saturday 5 February 1994, when a mortar attack on the city's market killed sixty-eight civilians and wounded hundreds. Outrage swept through Europe and North America.] This topic arose out of a seminar, 'The power of evil, the resistance of good', that took place at the Centro Studi Piero Gobetti on 8 June 1994. The seminar was promoted by Enrico Peyretti, editor of *Il Foglio*, a monthly periodical for Turinese Christians. The point of departure for the debate was provided by Aldo Bodrato's article 'Per non essere vinti dal male' ('So as not to be overwhelmed by evil'), published in the April issue. Drawing on the tragedy of the city of Sarajevo, 'ferita aperta nel cuore d'Europa' ('an open wound in the heart of Europe'), this proposed a reflection on Evil beyond religious apologetics and a critique based on the Enlightenment, noting that it was impossible not 'to capture

the equivalent of the late medieval nominalistic crisis in modern lay humanism and its nihilist crisis'. In the following issue, in May, in the article 'Non vince ma non può essere vinto' ('It does not win but cannot be overwhelmed'), referring to P. Ricoeur, 'Evil: a challenge to philosophy and theology', It. trs. I. Bertoletti (Brescia, Morcelliana 1993) now in his *Figuring the Sacred: Religion, Narrative, and Imagination* (Minneapolis, Fortress 1995), pp. 249–61, and also to L. Pareyson's *Filosofia della libertà* [*The Philosophy of Liberty*] (Genoa, Il Melangolo 1989), Peyretti invited us to reflect on the observation that 'what is extraordinary is not evil, but the fact that there is good and that it resists and persists'. At the seminar, both Bodrato and Pier Cesare Bori of the University of Bologna participated, and their papers were published in the July issue of *Il Foglio*.

2. S. Quinzio, *La sconfitta di Dio* [*God's Defeat*] (Milan, Adelphi 1992).

3. An example of natural evil so shocking as to prompt Darwin to write that he cannot be convinced that a benevolent and omnipotent God created it is the following. It refers to a swarm of wasps, no better defined, in which it happens that: 'The wasp deposits the eggs in the body of the caterpillar, but first it stings the poor creature's nervous system in order to completely paralyse it, but without killing it. Once the eggs hatch, the larvae feed on living flesh, guarding the vital centres of the victim until the end. The caterpillar is gradually lacerated from within, suffering atrociously, but unable to react as it cannot even move a muscle. Once the caterpillar is emptied there is nothing left to eat, and it is left to die.' I draw this passage from G. Toraldo di Francia, *Ex absurdo: Riflessioni di un fisico ottuagenario* [*Ex Absurdo: Reflections of an Octogenarian biologist*] (Milan, Feltrinelli 1991), pp. 42–3.

4. H. Jonas, 'The concept of God after Auschwitz: a Jewish voice', in his *Mortality and Morality: A Search for the Good After Auschwitz*, ed. Lawrence Vogel (Evanston IL, Northwestern University Press 1996), pp. 131–43. [Translator's note: The cited discussion is on pp. 139–40.]

Appendix

Understand Before Judging

I was surprised to read the following title on the first page of *l'Avvenire* (10 January 1989): 'Dear Professor, I am writing to you as a bishop.' The professor is me, the bishop, Monsignor Sandro Maggiolini. A surprise because, despite the numerous debates in which I have participated over the years, I have rarely, if ever, had such an authoritative interlocutor from the world of the church.

While I am not a man of faith, I have always held a high respect for believers. When faith is not a gift, it is a habit; when it is neither a gift nor a habit, it derives from a strong will to believe. Will, however, begins where reason ends, and until now I have stopped before that will to believe.

What is also completely foreign to me is to have faith in reason. I have never been tempted to substitute the God of believers with the Goddess of Reason. For me, our reason is not a beacon, but a small lamp. Nevertheless, we have no other guide to lead us in the darkness from which we began towards the darkness that awaits us. Many questions weigh upon us. How was the universe created? How will it end? What part does a human being play? This individual who, different from all the other living beings we know, is not only in the world but also questions his role in this world. To use the classical term of our whole tradition, he questions a destiny that is essentially 'blind'. Moreover, this individual finds himself steeped in the evil of the universe, or what he regards as evil, and from his extended reflections on the causes and aims, emerges the question 'Why evil?' A question to which he has never been able to provide a convincing answer.

I have no difficulty in admitting that science has not succeeded in this. By 'science' I mean the body of knowledge acquired by using our intelligence. But then, have religions succeeded? Here, I am referring to those convincing answers that can appease our intelligence, not to consolatory and therefore illusory answers. These serve only to gratify those individuals who, due to the enormity and intolerability of the evil they have to suffer, want desperately to be consoled.

Contrary to the small lamp of reason, faith illuminates, but often its dazzling light can cause blindness. From where, other than from this blindness, do the perverse aspects of religion emerge? Some examples are: intolerance, coercion to believe, persecution of non-believers, and a defiant spirit. I would not raise this old subject again were it not an identical argument constantly used with the same partisan spirit to attribute all the abuses of our century to the secularization process, as if the bloodiest age before the two world wars was not that of the wars of religion. Moreover, were one to ignore such a subject, it would be impossible to understand the struggle of the Enlightenment, so characteristic of modern thought.

I am happy to acknowledge that Monsignor Maggiolini, by exemplifying a deep sense of responsibility, rejects this spirit of 'revenge'. With a view to ending the useless and often hypocritical game of retaliation, he states that even 'If a certain type of Enlightenment is presently revealing its flaws, the church and Christians within it…do not have the right to claim any merit whatsoever.'

Given these premises, I reply briefly to the questions raised in that letter. First of all, confronted with the considered invitation extended to me and without any presumption of being less pessimistic, since pessimism, like optimism, is a global vision of the world and as such fideistic, I modestly regard myself as someone who tries to understand before judging. Starting from the observation of radical evil, what is important is that it is generally possible to maintain that the only antithesis to evil, the only attempt to overcome it, should be sought in the creation of moral life, because in this rests the uniqueness and novelty of the human world.

My reply to the question of whether we have reached the time when a justification of morals can be anchored to the Absolute is that the actual reason for anchoring morals to a religious vision does not rest in the need to provide an absolute basis for morals, but in the practical need to enforce its observance effectively. The appeal to God serves not so much to establish the rules that must be followed as to induce believers to obey them, irrespective of what they are. In other words, it appeals to God more as a judge (infallible and therefore more fearful than a human judge) than to God as legislator. The golden rule 'Do unto others what you would have them do unto you' exists in any rational kind of morals, including the utilitarian, which seems the most indifferent to religious morals.

The final question, 'What about lay people?', is the most embarrassing. The reason for this is quite simple: there is not only one set of lay morals (perhaps that is also the case for religious morals, but we shall not deal with this topic now). We read in the histories of philosophy that the ancients contrasted the ethics of virtue with the ethics of happiness. The moderns contrast the ethics of duty with the ethics of utility, not to mention the well-known Weberian distinction between the ethics of pure intention and the ethics of responsibility. The only principle considered intrinsically lay is that of tolerance. Based on the multiplicity of moral domains, this principle necessarily requires that ends and responsibility must coexist peacefully.

From this viewpoint, I have no fear in asserting that lay thought is an essential expression of the modern world, and an effect of the secularization process in which churches recognize themselves. Besides, as one can read in the pastoral constitution *Gaudium et Spes*: 'Respect and love must also be extended to those who think and act differently from us in social, political, and even religious matters. This is because the greater the humanity and love we apply in understanding their ways, the easier it will be for us to begin a dialogue with them.'

Clearly this coming together to dialogue represented by Monsignor Maggiolini's letter is a fine testimony for which I am grateful.

Free to Save
Ourselves

Sergio Quinzio's article 'Il pettine di Dio' ('God's comb'), published in *La Stampa* (11 February 1989), both stimulated and bewildered me.

The article places the subject of technology realistically before us, since it now seems to have eluded control of the human being, the sorcerer's apprentice. The subject is Heideggerian. Rather, it is that above all. To summarize: problems connected with the survival of humanity on the globe continue to increase, and are becoming much more serious. A threatening aspect is that they have no precedents. As such, seemingly they are without solutions.

The reasons for the lack of solutions are briefly the following:

1   The problems are so interconnected that by solving one another emerges.
2   There is no agreement on the possible remedies, so that we are becoming lost and generally disoriented.
3   The mass of problems is such that even when one is solved, it is merely a drop in the ocean.

So what now? These considerations are a further confirmation that the trust in boundless progress, which for centuries inspired various philosophies of history in the West, is exhausted. That trust rested on the idea that the evils humanity had suffered would find their remedy in the logical outcome of processes. War would be overcome through commerce and free exchange, and the spirit of enterprise would sweep away the spirit of conquest. Poverty would be eliminated by production, both in the capitalist version and in its opposite. Diseases would be eradicated through the advancement of medicine and the biological sciences. On the other hand, all this could similarly occur through a significant revolutionary movement that would overturn the traditional ways of producing and governing. In effect, Marx also evoked the image of the sorcerer's apprentice with regard to the triumphant bourgeoisie, but he envisaged the solution of the problem in the revolution of the expropriated against the expropriators.

Trust in progress has been shattered, on the one side, as a result of two world wars, the growing inequalities between the increasingly richer countries and the increasingly poorer countries, and the exploitative use of science and technology, also for evil purposes. On the other, that loss of trust resulted from the failure (also referred to as the 'suicide') of the revolution.

Since the faith of those, to use Quinzio's words, 'who see in the development of science and technology a kind of Apollonian lance, capable of simultaneously wounding and healing' has failed, we have begun to ask questions about the 'limits' of development. I would like, at least, to mention the posthumous book by Aurelio Peccei, one of the founders of the Club of Rome.[1] His central idea is that endless progress is on a collision course with the reality of a finite universe where humans must live. That universe is as extendable as human endeavour will allow, through the conquest of space and the more recent exploitation of the ocean bed, but nevertheless it is always finite.

Up to this point I fully agree with Quinzio. However, when one moves from diagnosis to remedies, this is where the stimulation ends and the bewilderment begins. Reconsidering Heidegger's famous statement in his last interview, published posthumously in *Der Spiegel*,[2] Quinzio argues that he is convinced the only solution rests with those individuals who believe that 'after all this only a God can save us'. Ever since this phrase was revealed, I have asked myself whether Wittgenstein's 'silence' is not more consistent with the essence of philosophy than Heidegger's answer, which is vague and banal. Should we not have the right to expect something more than this resigned appeal of the afflicted, of the humiliated, and of those who have no rest due to their tribulations, from the greatest philosopher of this century, or, even for those who do not regard him as such, from the most influential?

I now ask the same question. Clearly, I ask it first of myself, of my indomitable incredulity, even in the face of such authoritative judgment. Foremost, why 'a God' (*ein Gott*), and not 'God'? It is inevitable that when someone indicates 'a God' our quite limited faculty of reasoning is immediately prompted to ask a first question: 'Which God?' Another follows directly, suggested by our historical experience, also limited, but this is the only one we have that enables us to provide sensible answers: 'When has a God ever saved the world?' For believers, Christ came to save humankind from sin and earthly death. He did not come to save the world, which was not his kingdom. This is the world with all its splendours (the 'starry sky' mentioned by Kant), and with all its faults (the earthquakes that swallow whole cities, the storm that indiscriminately destroys trees and houses). Throughout our known history, and as far as we are aware until now, humans have saved themselves, when they have, and condemned themselves, when they have, on their own. Who saved them from the plague? Who condemned them to exterminate their kind in the far-away Americas, and close by, even in time, in Germany?

There are those who may well object and say: 'You cannot deduce plausible arguments from what has happened to make a judgment about what will, or could, happen. You cannot preclude hope.'

I do not preclude hope, since I do not have, among other things, any certainty about the future. I do not have, however, the least uncertainty in thinking that to entrust ourselves only to hope without a premonitory sign, even in a prophetic history of humanity such as that considered by Kant, can lead to resignation, or to passive waiting, or to even not attempting to do, as Quinzio himself conceded, 'what little one can and where one can'.

Finally, even suspending judgment on the 'if', I cannot prevent an even more disturbing question from surfacing in my mind: 'Why?' Why should a God save the world? Why? In the universe of unlimited worlds, who are we? What merits do we claim? We are so intelligent as to understand evil, but at the same time we are so stupid as to be unable to find the remedy by ourselves. Why should someone who is not responsible for our misadventures save us?[3]

Quinzio concluded by citing Kierkegaard's apologue, according to which 'the world will perish amid the universal amusement of creative people'. I also have my citation: 'We run carelessly over the precipice after having erected a barrier to prevent ourselves from seeing it' (Pascal, *Pensées*, 342). But is not our repeating with Heidegger 'only a God can save us' perhaps a sign of this 'carefree' attitude?

Notes

1. A. Peccei, and I. Daisaku, *Campanello d'allarme per il XXI secolo* (*An Alarm Bell for the Twenty-first Century*) (Milan, Bompiani 1985). Peccei earlier stressed that 'our oneness with nature is the primary element of our being to . . . [and] is the basic imperative of our age': A. Peccei and I. Daisaku, *Before it is Too Late* (London, Macdonald 1984), pp. 18, 32.
2. M. Heidegger, 'Ormai solo un Dio ci può salvare' ('After all this only a God can save us'), interviewed in *Der Spiegel* (Milan, Guanda 1987).
3. In an article 'Formaggio e diritti umani' ('Cheese and human rights'), Salman Rushdie wrote: 'There are no longer gods to help us. We are alone. Stated differently, we are free. The drift away from the divine has placed us at the centre of the land-scape, where we need to build our morals and our communities, make our choices and act according to our principles. Once again, at the dawn of the idea of Europe we find an emphasis on what is human. Gods can come and go, but we move onward endlessly. For me, this humanistic emphasis is one of the most attractive features of European thought': *La Stampa*, 5 February 1996.

Note about the Texts

The first edition of this book emerged from Santina Mobiglia and Pietro Polito's idea of publishing my unpublished conference paper on 'Meekness', given a few years earlier, in *Linea d'ombra*, under the editorship of Goffredo Fofi. Compared with the range of my books, it was a self-indulgent piece. But was it such an isolated case, after all, as not to find others that were similar among the numerous pages I had written over many years? The two explorers and editors of that piece searched among my old and new papers to the extent that a year later they managed to put together a small collection of moral writings, which Fofi offered the readers of his journal, publishing it in the series 'Aperture' ['Openings'], also edited by him.

The book presented in the series 'Nuovi Saggi' by Pratiche Editrice has been substantially updated from the preceding edition. I have added the bibliographic references and taken into account some critical reactions prompted by the first edition, and certain debates on the same topics that had emerged in the meantime. I rearranged the chapters to make their flow more coherent, removed repetitive pages, and transferred others to the appendix. Finally, I added a new chapter on 'Tolerance and truth', alongside 'Truth and liberty'. Above all, I included an extended introduction, reflecting on the various themes, and connecting them in order to provide a more unitary form to the collection. I also respond to some criticisms and comments.

'In Praise of Meekness' emerged from a conference held in Milan on 8 March 1983, in the ambit of the cycle 'Piccolo

dizionario delle virtù' ['A small dictionary of virtues'], promoted by Ernesto Treccani through the initiative of the fon-
dazione Corrente. Under the editorship of Santina Mobiglia
and Pietro Polito it was published for the first time in December 1993 as a supplement to *Linea d'ombra*. It was translated
into English with the title 'In Praise of Meekness' by Teresa
Chataway, with the Italian text alongside, in the first issue of
Convivio: Journal of Ideas in Italian Studies (1995) I (1), pp.
21–38; in French, 'Eloge de la mitezza', by Pierre-Emmanuel
Danzat, for the special issue of *Diogène*, devoted to *La tolérance entre l'intolérance et l'intolérable* [*Tolerance between intolerance and the intolerable*] (1996), 166, October–December,
pp. 3–17; as 'In praise of la mitezza' in the English edition of
Diogène (1996), 44/4 (176), Winter, pp. 3–18. The whole
book was published in Spanish as *Elogio de la templanza y otros
escritos morales: Estudio preliminar* by Rafael de Asís Roig, tr.
Francisco Javier Ansuátegui Roig (Madrid, Ediciones Temas
de Hoy 1997).

'Ethics and politics' combines 'Etica e politica' in [Aa. Vv.]
various authors, *Etica e politica*, ed. Walter Tega (Parma, Pratiche 1984), pp. 7–17, and 'Etica e politica', *MicroMega*
(1986), 4, pp. 97–118. Now, in annotated form, in N. Bobbio,
Elementi di politica: Antologia [*Fundamental Principles of Politics: An Anthology*], ed. P. Polito (Milan, Einaudi Scuola 1998).

'Reason of state and democracy' appeared under the title
'Morale e politica' in *Nuova Antologia* (1991), 2179, July–
September, pp. 67–79.

'The nature of prejudice' in [Aa. Vv.] various authors, *La
natura del pregiudizio* (Turin, Piedmont Region n.d.), pp.
2–15. This is the text of a lecture on 'La natura del pregiudizio' delivered in a course held at the Instituto tecnico indus-
triale Amedeo Avogadro di Torino from 5 November to 17
December 1979. The course was part of the programme
'Turin Encyclopedia – The Culture of the City'.

'Racism today' in *Scuola e Città* (1993), XLIV (4), 30
April, pp. 179–83. This is the text prepared for a conference
on the topic of racism held at SERMIG in Turin during
December 1992. Published in part in *La Stampa* (1992), 27
December, under the title 'Gli italiani sono razzisti?' ['Are

Italians racist?']. Republished in *Nuova Antologia* (1993), 2186, April–June, in a series of articles under the title 'Razzismo, xenofobia, antisemitismo in Europa' ['Racism, xenophobia, anti-Semitism in Europe'], pp. 6–10. Republished as 'Racism today' in *Sisifo*, Ideas, studies and programmes of the Istituto Gramsci piemontese, October 1993 (Quaderno 1, 'Against prejudice', in collaboration with CGIL Scuola/ Torino Valore Scuola).

'Truth and liberty' was an introductory paper at the XVIIIth National Congress of the Società filosofica italiana, Palermo–Messina, 18–22 March 1960, and later in [Aa. Vv.] various authors, *Verità e libertà* [*Truth and Liberty*] (Palermo, Palumbo 1960), 1, pp. 43–52.

'Tolerance and truth' is the rewriting of some of my pieces on tolerance, in particular that published in *Lettera internazionale* (1988), v (15), January–March, pp. 16–18, and included in my *Il dubbio e la scelta: Intellettuali e potere nelle società contemporanee* [*The Doubt and the Choice: Intellectuals and Power in Contemporary Societies*] (Rome, La Nuova Italia Scientifica 1993), pp. 207–12.

'For and against lay ethics' in *Il Mulino* (1983), XXXIII (2), March–April, pp. 159–72. A revised text of the conference held at Bologna, for the Martedì del Convento di San Domenico, on 18 October 1983.

'The gods that failed': a revised and edited transcription of the paper presented at the seminar 'Il potere del male, la resistenza del bene' ['The power of evil, and the strength of good'], held at the Centro Studi Piero Gobetti di Torino, 8 June 1994.

'Understand before judging' appeared as 'Sulla vita morale: Bobbio risponde al vescovo' ['On moral life: Bobbio's reply to the bishop'], *La Stampa* (1989), 14 January.

'Free to save ourselves' (Bobbio's response to Sergio Quinzio): *La Stampa* (1989), 17 February.

Index